Handmade bags

Handmade
bags

Terence
Terry

SEARCH PRESS

A QUARTO BOOK

Published in 2003 by Search Press Ltd
Wellwood
North Farm Road
Tunbridge Wells
Kent TN2 3DR
United Kingdom

Originally published in paperback
by A&C Black, 2002

Copyright © 2002 Quarto plc.

ISBN 1-903975-99-9

QUAR.BAGS

Conceived, designed, and produced by
Quarto Publishing plc
The Old Brewery
6 Blundell St
London N7 9BH

Senior Project Editor Nicolette Linton
Senior Art Editor Elizabeth Healey
Text Editors Jean Coppendale, Alice Tyler
Designer Julie Francis
Illustrators Terry Evans, Carol Mula, Kate
Simunek
Assistant Art Director Penny Cobb
Photographer Colin Bowling
Indexer Pamela Ellis

Art Director Moira Clinch
Publisher Piers Spence

Manufactured by Universal Graphics, Singapore
Printed by Midas Printing International
Limited, China

9 8 7 6 5 4 3 2 1

Author's Acknowledgements
With special thanks to Katie for designing
a range of beautiful bags through the eyes
of a jeweller, and to Caroline Darke for her
fabulous bag on page 90.

conte

The essentials

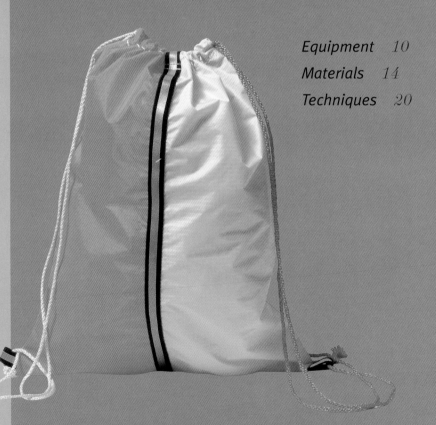

nts

The bags 32

Introduction

*a*ccessories can make or break an outfit, and a handbag can provide that special finishing touch to whatever you're wearing. Not since the late 1960s have handbags been so popular; people have taken to bags with a passion. So whether you are after a sturdy shopper or an exotic and glamorous evening bag, it makes sense to create your own bag to reflect your individual style.

Bags are much simpler to make than you might think. You probably already have most of the equipment at home in your sewing basket, and some of the designs in this book can be made without a sewing machine. Use offcuts of fabrics from clothes or soft furnishing projects, and check out your

jewellery case for odds and ends you never wear. Most objects – even galvanized wire and rubber tubing – can be recycled to make a unique bag for you or for your friends.

This book begins with a look at the essential equipment, materials and techniques that you will need to make these bags, and we will show you how to use the patterns for each design (see pages 20–21).

The section on bags contains 30 projects, each one explained in simple illustrated steps, with tips from the author. Beginning with embellishments to shop-bought bags, this section also includes a couple of makeovers to revitalise old favourites. The next section introduces designs for bags that are simple to make and require only basic skills. More challenging projects follow, including those that include simple knitting and crochet. Finally, some advanced projects explain how to insert zips and pockets, how to work with an advanced quilting pattern, and how to use real and fake leather, as well as a range of furnishing fabrics.

Happy handbagging!

Many of the bags in this book have been made with basic sewing techniques – some of the designs can even be created without a sewing machine. Before you start, check your sewing kit. You will find that you already have much of the equipment that you need to make the designs in this book: pins, needles, thread and scissors, for starters. Don't discount the more unusual materials, such as fabric offcuts, costume jewellery and household materials. The fun in making your own bags comes from using your imagination and creating something from nothing!

The essenti

equipment

Before you start

It's a good idea to collect together in advance some essential tools that you will need, regardless of the bag you plan to make or embellish. A well-stocked sewing kit will help you to work more quickly and efficiently.

Sewing machine

Pins

Needle and thread

SEWING MACHINE

A sewing machine is faster and easier to use than stitching by hand. Modern machines provide simple, useful stitches such as straight stitch, zigzag and reverse stitch that can also be quite decorative. It is advisable to use attachments for bindings, a zip foot and Teflon feet when working with plastic or leather.

Before sewing, check that the bobbin is loaded with the correct thread and also check the stitch tensions and length on a spare piece of doubled fabric.

STEAM IRON AND IRONING BOARD

A steam iron should be used throughout the process of making your bag, not only at the final stages. Always iron or press fabrics first before cutting out the pattern. The base of the iron should be kept clean and the ironing board fitted with a padded cover that should be cleaned or changed regularly.

NEEDLES AND PINS

Always use sharp, stainless steel pins as these will not rust. For finer fabrics, use lace pins. Pins with glass heads are useful as they can be seen easily on fabric – plastic heads will melt if they come in contact with your iron. You will need an assortment of needles for hand sewing and for your machine in your sewing tool kit. There is a wide range of needles available for use with different types and thickness of fabric.

For hand sewing, needles come in different lengths, numbered sizes, eye sizes and fineness. These include betweens, sharps, embroidery/crewels and darners. Sizes range from 1 to 24 – the smaller the number of the needle, the shorter and thicker it is. For embroidery there are three basic types: crewel, chenille and tapestry. Each one has a particular use, and the choice of needle depends on the embroidery technique being worked.

Machine needles should also be chosen according to the type and thickness of fabric that you are using. These needles are numbered by size and lettered to indicate the shape of the tip, and they should be changed regularly.

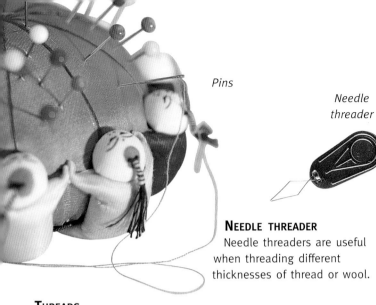

Pins

Needle threader

NEEDLE THREADER
Needle threaders are useful when threading different thicknesses of thread or wool.

THREADS
It is worth paying a little more for good quality thread. Cheap thread will break and fray with use. It is also important to match the thread with your fabric exactly. Many types of threads are available according to the type of fabric and its thickness. Tacking thread is far easier to break than sewing threads, and comes in a range of colours, not just in black and white.

THIMBLE
A thimble is useful when tacking, hand stitching or decorative stitching. A metal thimble provides the best protection.

Thimbles

SCISSORS

You will need different types of scissors – a pair for cutting paper only, a pair of sharp dressmaking scissors for fabric only and a pair of small embroidery scissors for detailed work and for trimming threads.

You will also need a pair of pinking shears. These can be used for neatening seams and for decorative edges when working with non-grain materials such as leather, suede, felt and plastics.

TRACING PAPER

Tracing paper is usually waxed on one side and may be coloured white, red, blue or yellow. It is used for drafting patterns from a grid when enlarging.

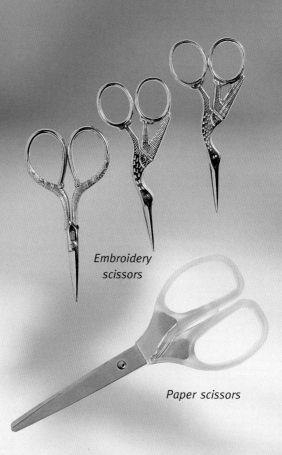

Embroidery scissors

Paper scissors

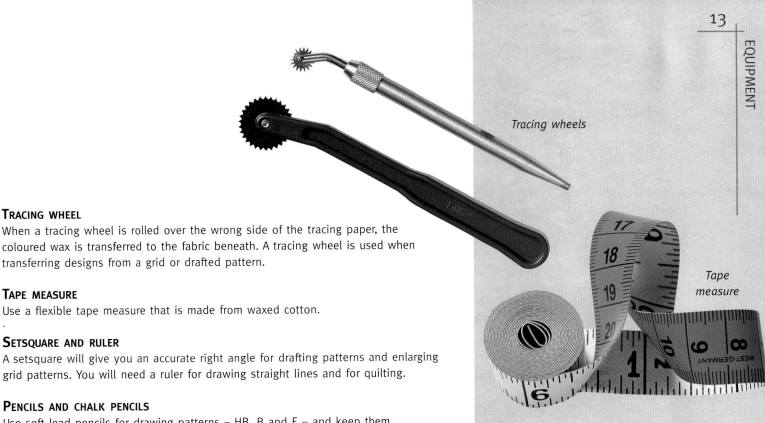

Tracing wheels

TRACING WHEEL

When a tracing wheel is rolled over the wrong side of the tracing paper, the coloured wax is transferred to the fabric beneath. A tracing wheel is used when transferring designs from a grid or drafted pattern.

TAPE MEASURE

Use a flexible tape measure that is made from waxed cotton.

SETSQUARE AND RULER

A setsquare will give you an accurate right angle for drafting patterns and enlarging grid patterns. You will need a ruler for drawing straight lines and for quilting.

PENCILS AND CHALK PENCILS

Use soft lead pencils for drawing patterns – HB, B and F – and keep them sharpened. Chalk pencils can be used to make quick marks on the fabric that can be brushed away on completion.

TAILOR'S CHALK

Tailor's chalk is used for drawing around the paper pattern onto the wrong side of the fabric.

WEIGHTS

Small metal weights can be used when working with delicate fabrics as pins may easily mark the fabric.

Place the weights on the pattern to secure its place over the fabric. Draw around the entire shape with tailor's chalk.

Tape measure

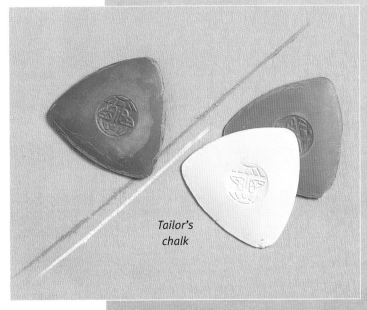

Tailor's chalk

Leather and
fake fur

Knitted wool

fabrics

Before you buy

Having decided to make your own bag, you now have to choose your fabric. The choices are almost endless – from leather and suede to denim and felt, from velvet and silk to rubber and metal fibre fabrics.

Of course, the type of bag that you want to make and what you plan to use it for will influence your choice. If you want a bag for everyday use or for shopping trips then a strong, hardwearing material such as heavy-duty cotton, suede or leather is ideal. But if you want a pretty, sophisticated evening bag for occasional use, then a lighter fabric such as satin, silk or organza would be more appropriate.

At the shop

The colour and pattern of the fabric is a matter of personal preference and may depend on your budget. Some fabrics require special stitching or pressing because of their structure or finish, so it is worth asking about any special requirements before buying. Other fabrics need careful handling, and may involve more time or expertise. For example, leather, taffeta and metallic fabrics can be stitched only once – removed stitches will leave holes. Silks and slinky fabrics are difficult to cut and handle while sewing. It is also worth remembering that small prints, especially dark colours, hide any stitching imperfections, are easier to sew and require no pattern matching. Fabrics are sold at standard widths that will be large enough to accommodate the handbag patterns in this book: 90cm (36 in) for cottons, silks, satins, and 140cm (54 in) for wool, felt and furnishing fabrics.

If you want your bag to complement a particular outfit, wear the outfit or take it to the fabric shop to check that the colour matches or contrast works well. Finally, check the raw edges of your chosen fabric for excessive fraying. If it frays badly, allow 5mm (¼ in) extra on the seam allowances when cutting out.

Rayon

Quilted silk

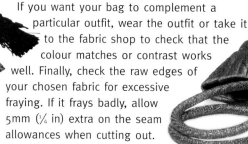

Indian silk

Light-use fabrics

FUN FUR OR FAKE FUR

Fun or fake furs, usually acrylic, are made to resemble real animal fur. They may be dyed different shades and patterns, and also are sold in strips for trimming.

VELVET

Velvet is a fabric with a short, closely woven pile made from silk, cotton and synthetics. It has a soft texture and lustrous, rich appearance. Common types include:
Velveteen – similar to velvet, nearly always made from cotton.
Crushed velvet – pile is pressed flat in one or several directions, making it shimmer.
Panne – pile is flattened in one direction to give a lustrous sheen. Often available with printed designs as well as plain colours, and is both stretchable and washable.

Tip

When stitching together velvet or other pile fabrics such as synthetic furs, the pile should lie in the same direction. Stitch in the direction of the pile. After stitching, pull the pile out of the seam with the point of a pin.

SATIN

Satin is a sleek fabric with a lustrous sheen.

Tip

When working with slippery fabrics such as satin, place a layer of tissue paper between the two layers to be sewn. The tissue will help them grip together enough to sew. Simply remove the tissue after you have completed the seam.

SILK

Silk fabrics have a sheen and are lightweight. They have a delicate appearance, but are quite strong.

METALLIC FABRICS (LAMÉ, LUREX)

Metallic fabrics are available in stunning colours and textures. If the fabric you choose is flimsy, strengthen it with iron-on interfacing.

Tips

Stitching – Any metallic fabric can be stitched only once as removed stitches will leave holes. Use a very fine needle and change it regularly.
Pressing – Use a dry iron at a low temperature; steam may tarnish metallic fabric. Open seams with the tip of the iron and, elsewhere, use a pressing cloth with only light pressure.

Other light-use fabrics include: sateen, taffeta, voile, velour, gauze, lawn and organdy.

Fake fur

Velvet

Silks, satins, lace and beaded fabrics

Metallic fabrics

Corduroy

Furnishing fabrics

Wire mesh

Felt

Hard-wearing fabrics

LEATHER

There are many synthetic fabrics that imitate leather. Common names include buckskin, patent and suede.

Tip

Stitching – Leather can be stitched only once as any removed stitches leave holes. Wedge-point needles should be used; these penetrate the leather and minimize tearing. Use a specially coated presser foot to prevent the leather from sticking. Pressing – Seams should be pressed open, using fingers or a dry iron set at a low temperature. Adhesive may be required to hold seam allowances flat.

SUEDE CLOTH

Suede cloth is a woven or knitted fabric of cotton, wool, artificial fibres or blends, usually napped and shorn to resemble suede.

COTTON

Cotton comes in a vast range of weights from flimsy muslin and lace to canvas and blankets. Cotton is often blended with other fibres to enhance its qualities such as strength and moisture absorbency.

FELT

Felt is a non-woven fabric comprised of wool, fur or hair fibres that have been meshed together by heat, moisture and mechanical action. Felt is not a strong fabric and can tear easily.

DENIM

Denim is a strong, hard-wearing twill-weave cotton or cotton-blend fabric.

CORDUROY

A heavy cotton, ribbed pile fabric, corduroy has a smooth velvet-like nap.

Other hard-wearing fabrics include canvas, brocade, vinyl, worsted, frieze, hessian, moleskin and furnishing fabrics such as chintz.

Novelty materials

From bright green plastic turf (see pages 50-51) to wire mesh and rubber tubing (see pages 54-57), there is an amazing range of outrageous and extraordinary materials available for your new bag. A visit to your local hardware store or even to a garden centre may give you some brilliant ideas. Just let your imagination run rampant and experiment with different materials, textures and colours.

embellishments

A well-placed glass droplet, bright beads, scattered sequins or tassels can give a professional finish to a newly completed bag or revitalise a tired old bag. Dig deep into the corners of your jewellery box and sewing bag. There are no limits when it comes to embellishing, so use your imagination.

SEQUINS AND BEADS
Sequins and beads can be used to create stunning single motifs. Sequins can be applied so that the stitches show or so they are hidden (see left). If you want them to show, choose an attractive twisted silk or stranded embroidery cotton.

Beads can be applied individually or in a continuous line (see left). The stitches should not show on the right side of the fabric. Some beads have only a tiny hole, so you may need a special beading needle to stitch them in place. Use a fine, strong thread, and secure the beginning and end of the thread firmly.

TRIMMINGS
Contrasting braids, cords, fringes or ribbons can be used as finishing touches. When buying trimmings, add a bit extra to the length for experiments, turning corners and joining lengths. Trimmings can be added into a seam at the construction stage, or slip stitched by hand when you have finished your bag.

HANDLES
Handles can also be used as embellishments. Twisted rubber, plaited cord or ethnic necklaces, can add to the unique finish of your bag. Or look out for old bags in the attic or at garage sales – just remove the handles and attach them to your bag.

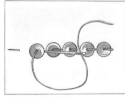

Applying sequins with the stitches showing

Applying sequins with invisible stitches

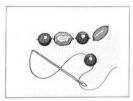

Stitching individual beads

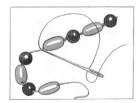

Stitching beads in a continuous line

linings
and facings

A good lining will give a neat, finished look to your bag and will also hide any untidy seams and edges. Linings should be chosen with almost as much care as the main fabric of your handbag. Your choice of lining material will depend on the type of bag you are making and also on the type of main fabric that you are using. A shopping bag will need a strong lining, which is easily cleaned. But for an exotic evening bag, you could have a shiny, silky fabric such as satin, which will complement the general effect of your bag.

Remember, whenever you open your bag the lining is on display. And so the colour and texture should be in keeping with the main fabric of the bag – avoid clashing colours or strongly contrasting patterns unless that is the look you want. Don't think that you can reuse old scraps of leftover material to line your bag – this is a big mistake.

The lining seams are sewn in the same way as the seams of the main fabric. Press open the lining's seam allowances and leave the zip area open with seam allowances pressed back. Hand stitch the seam allowances of the lining along both sides of the zip tape.

FABRICS

Linings come in a wide range of lightweight materials such as silk, satin, taffeta and rayon. They should be smooth, opaque and durable, and ideally with an anti-static finish.

Iron-on facings

Facings are often forgotten or deliberately left out of many home sewing projects because they are considered unnecessary. But facings, and iron-on varieties in particular, are important, as they will give support and rigidity to the main fabric and design of your bag. Generally, the more structured and detailed your design is, the greater need there is to include good, iron-on facings. They will add to the overall finish and appearance of your handbag, even though they are 'behind the scenes'.

Always apply the facing before inserting the lining. Facings will help to give shape to your bag, and also support and stabilize specific areas such as cuffs, flaps, hems and edges. They will also prevent stretching.

Facings can be light, medium or heavy in weight and should be compatible with the main fabric of your bag. Iron-on facings are generally recommended for use on fabrics that can withstand high iron temperatures. Use a damp pressing cloth when applying iron-on facing. Fusing time is generally between 10 and 20 seconds.

FACINGS

1 Fusible woven interlining – adds extra thickness and body to fabric.
2 Fusible non-woven interlining – soft and firm synthetic fibre.
3 Flat domette – black or white fabric suitable for mounting silk, satin and cottons.
4 Wadding – synthetic fabric for a padded effect mainly for quilting.
5 Felt – to give extra body and firmness in stitch detailing.
6 Buckram – white fabric with a coarse grain giving a rigid effect.
7 Fusible canvas – suitable for thicker fabrics for a tailored look.
8 Vilene – fusible and non-fusible, used for simple, easy styling.
9 Acetate by the sheet – mainly used for strengthening the base of the bag.

Tips

• The softer or lighter in weight the main fabric is, the more support it will need from iron-on facings.
• Always use sew-in facings for fabrics such as velvet, fake fur, synthetic leather, mesh and vinyl.
• Iron-on or fusible facings have a shiny resin or "sugary" appearance on the side that bonds with the fabric.
• Test a small piece of iron-on facing with a small piece of your fabric before applying the main facing.
• Use a dark facing on dark fabrics.

*t*he quickest way to create a mess or end up with a disaster is to miss out on the planning stage. Many of the designs in this book have a pattern attached, and it is essential to understand how these work and their importance to successful bag making.

making and using a pattern

The grid of the pattern shows one square as 5cm (2 inches). Follow the steps on the following page to find out how to scale up the pattern and use it to cut out your fabric. Remember that the materials and equipment list for each design is specific to the size of bag the author has made. You will need to measure the fabric for your bag accordingly.

Grain: *direction of warp on fabric*
Warp: *threads running from top to bottom*
Weft: *threads running from left to right*

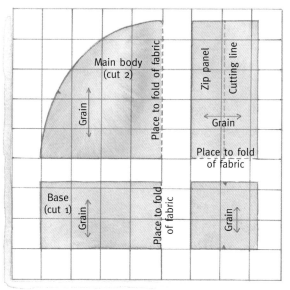

Main body (cut 2)

Grain

Place to fold of fabric

Zip panel

Cutting line

Grain

Place to fold of fabric

Base (cut 1)

Grain

Place to fold of fabric

Grain

EQUIPMENT

- Paper
- Pencil
- Tailor's chalk
- Ruler
- Scissors
- Pins
- Needle
- Bright thread

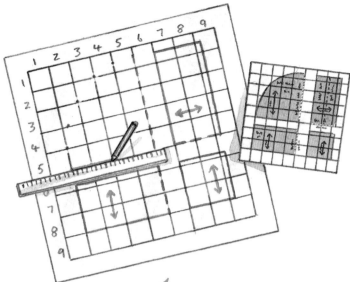

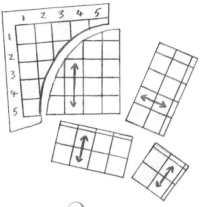

1 Scale up the pattern: count the squares on the pattern and draw it up on paper to the actual size of the bag you wish to make – one square equals 5cm (2 inches).

2 Using scissors, carefully cut out your pattern.

3 Pin the pattern onto the fabric. Draw a line around the pattern using tailor's chalk to mark it onto the fabric.

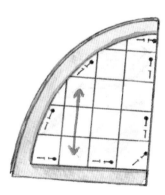

4 Cut out the fabric, leaving an extra 2.5cm (1 inch) for a seam allowance.

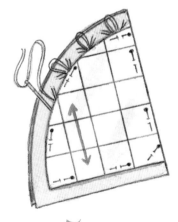

5 Make some tailor tacks around the edge of the pattern to show where the stitch line is.

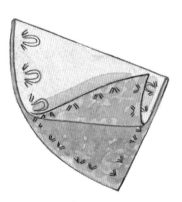

6 Pull off the pattern, and clip through the tailor tacks, leaving tack tufts on both pieces of fabric.

Tip: To make sure your tailor tacks don't drop out, use bright thread to stitch around the sewing line and leave a tail at least 12mm (½ inch) long at each end.

basic hand stitches

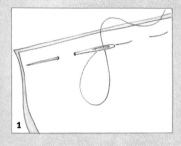

Tacking

Use the tacking stitch to hold and join two pieces of fabric together before sewing. Prior to tacking, pin the fabric with right sides together. Knot the thread at one end.

1. As shown above, stitch evenly along the seam line, using stitches about 5mm ($\frac{1}{4}$ in) in length. After machine sewing the seam, remove the tacking stitches.

Tailor's tacks

Tailor's tacks (see left) are used when transferring pattern lines to a double layer of fabric. Use a double length of thread in a contrasting color.

1. To begin, make a stitch through the double-layered fabric, pull the thread through, leaving about 1.5mm ($\frac{1}{12}$ in) length of thread on the top side. Insert the needle again into the first point of the stitch and pull through to form a loop of thread. Continue all around the pattern.

2. When completed, carefully cut through the loops. Ease the two layers of fabric apart and snip the under threads. Gently open out the two fabrics and you will have a thread mark of each piece of fabric.

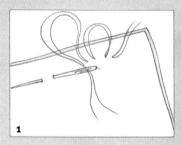

Quick tailor's tacks

To make quick tailor's tacks, use a double thread in a contrasting color from the fabric you are using.

1. With a large tacking stitch work around the pattern.

2. When completed, snip into the thread at the center.

3. Open the two fabrics and snip the under threads.

Back stitch

To make back stitches, you'll be working from left to right.

1. Bring out the needle at point (A), then insert the needle at point (B) coming out at point (C) at an equal distance.

2. Repeat for the next stitch with the needle entering at point (B).

3. The needle should enter the point made by the third emerging stitch from point (A) of the previous stitch.

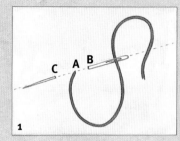

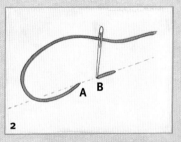

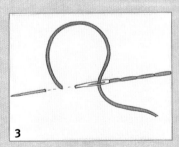

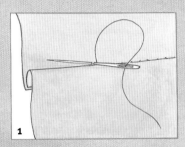

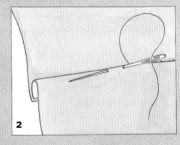

Slip stitch

Slip stitch is mainly used when sewing in linings or hemming by hand.

1. Begin by running the needle through the folded edge of the lining. Bring the needle out and pick up a couple of threads from the above fabric.

2. Return the needle into the folded edge and repeat until complete. Fasten off any loose threads and lose the thread through the fabric.

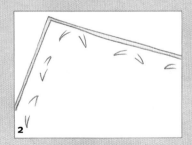

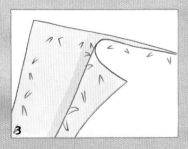

decorative hand stitches

Decorative stitches can be used sparingly for a subtle finish, or more obviously to highlight a particular feature. Use one type of stitch for low-key impact, or a range of stitches for a unique and special finish. Blanket stitch, feather stitch and many different embroidery stitches can all be used to enhance the loveliness of your bag. However, always ensure that the stitches complement the type and style of bag you have made, and that they are suitable for the weight of fabric.

Tips
- Crewel or chenille needles are used to embroider fabric. They have larger eyes than ordinary sewing needles to accommodate a thicker thread.
- Crewel needles are used for fine and medium-weight embroidering.
- Chenille needles are suitable for use with heavier threads and fabrics.
- Always use a fine needle if you are embroidering on a light, delicate fabric.

Blanket stitch

Blanket stitch is ideal to use around the edges of appliqué shapes, for hemming, or as a decorative stitch in embroidery. It can also be used as a buttonhole stitch if worked closely. The stitches should be evenly spaced and equal in length.

1. First bring the needle up through the fabric at point (A).
2. Then bring the needle down at point (B).
3. Lastly, bring it up again at point (C), with the thread under the needle. Pull the needle through to form a loop.

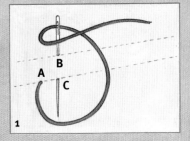

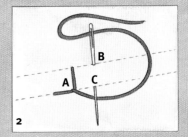

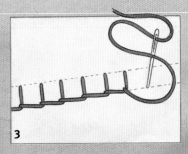

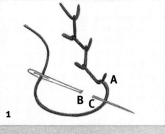

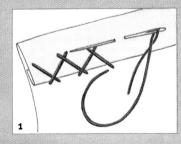

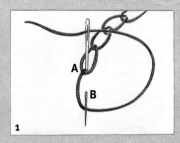

Chain stitch

Chain stitch forms a line on plain- and even-weave fabrics. Chain stitch can be used as an outline stitch, and is very useful for defining curves and intricate shapes.
1. Working vertically, bring the needle out at point (A), insert it back in the same place, and bring it out again at point (B), taking the thread under the point of the needle before pulling it through.

Herringbone stitch

The herringbone stitch can be used on plain- and even-weave fabrics to make an attractive, crossed zigzag line. It makes a rich border, particularly if a metallic thread is used for the interlacing. It is used for catching up hems and as a decorative embroidery stitch.
1. Working from left to right, take small stitches from *right* to *left*, first at the top and then at the bottom.

Feather stitch

The feather stitch is a decorative embroidery stitch that is often worked over a seamline in patchwork or appliqué where a series of stitches are worked on alternate sides of a given line. Mark the line the stitching is to follow on the right side of the fabric.
1. Working from top to bottom, bring the needle out at point (A), insert it at point (B), and bring it out again at point (C), taking the thread under the point of the needle before pulling it through. Repeat in reverse at the other side.

Other decorative stitches include stem stitch, couching stitch, French knots, satin stitch and cross stitch.

machine stitches

Before beginning any machine stitching, remember the golden rules:
- Check the tension on your machine, and use the correct machine foot.
- Practice on a small piece of fabric first to test the combination of needle, thread, and stitch length.
- Have plenty of new, sharp needles on hand.

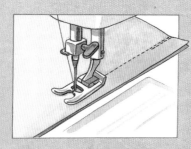

Back stitch

The back stitch is used to secure the beginning and end of a row of machine stitching. Back stitching eliminates the need to tie thread ends.

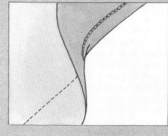

Chain stitch

Available on some machines, the chain stitch consists of a series of interlocking stitches made from a single thread. It is made by fitting a chain stitch needleplate. The upper thread twists around the empty bobbin case and the bobbin thread is not used.

Blind-hemming stitch

Also named blind stitch, this zigzag stitch pattern is used primarily for blind hemming by machine. It can also be used to stitch seams and to finish seams (see Seams on pages 28–29).

For fabrics that do not fray easily, such as woollens and jerseys, it is not necessary to fold under the hem edge. The hem allowance is left flat before being folded back for stitching. The stitch pattern usually comprises 4 to 6 straight stitches followed by 1 zigzag. Some machines form a blind stitch comprising several narrow zigzag stitches followed by 1 wider zigzag.

To blind-hem stitch fabrics that fray, it is necessary to fold under the hem edge before stitching, as shown below. This ensures that the raw edge of the hem is enclosed with the hem allowance.

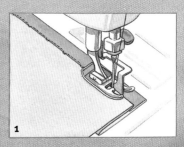

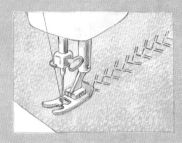

Feather stitch

The feather stitch is decorative as well as practical and it can be used for faggoting, embroidery or quilting. Feather stitch, when used at o stitch width, may also be used for the straight reverse stitch. This stitch may either be built into your machine or can be produced by the insertion of a separate stitch pattern cam.

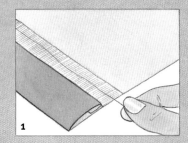

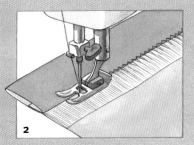

Hem stitch

Fully automatic machines have built-in hem stitching capabilities; others can produce hem stitching through the insertion of special cams. Decorative hemming is a process which can be created in the fabric by the use of a wing needle. The best fabrics for using wing needles are very fine fabrics such as organza or lawn.
1. Fold up the hem allowance and turn under the hem edge. Draw threads of fabric from above the hem edge.
2. Zigzag along both edges of the drawn-thread section.

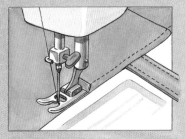

Top stitch

Machine stitches made from the right side of the fabric for decorative or functional reasons, sometimes both, is called top stitching. This is usually a plain straight stitch, set at a longer than usual stitch length. It is sometimes advisable to tighten the top tension for this stitch. The thread can be ordinary sewing thread or a heavier thread such as a silk buttonhole twist. The thread color can match or contrast, according to the effect you want to achieve.

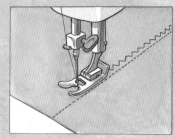

Zigzag stitch

For any zigzag stitching, always use a zigzag foot. Consult your machine manual for the best stitch settings.

Tip
Machine needles have different points designed for various fabric weights. The most commonly used are sharp-point for woven fabrics, ball-point for stretchy fabrics, extra fine points for twill, denim and heavy linens, and wedge-points for leather and vinyls. The finer the weight of the fabric and thread being used, the finer the needle should be.

seams

Finished seams add a professional touch to any bag. They help to neaten edges and stop them from fraying. Plain seams help to create the shape of your bag and should be almost invisible when pressed. Decorative seams emphasize the lines of shaping and are often used as a strong design feature. The choice of seam will depend on the weight of the fabric you are using and the purpose of the bag you are making. The machine should be adjusted correctly to the fabric for stitch length, tension and pressure. Seams should be back stitched at the beginning and end for reinforcement.

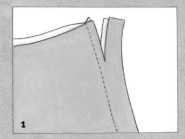

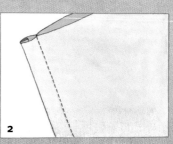

Constructing a seam

To construct a basic seam:
1. Pin the seam at regular intervals, matching the pattern's notches and other markings. Place the pins perpendicular to the seamline, with the heads toward the seam edge. Tack close to the seam line, removing the pins as you go. With many simple seams pinning and machine stitching is sufficient.

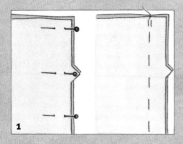

2. Position the needle in the seamline, 1cm (⅜ in) from the end. Stitch forward along the seamline, close to but not through the tacking. Remove any pins as you stitch. Remove all tacking stitches. Press the seam flat in the direction it was stitched, then press it open.

Special seams are used for particular types of fabric. A velvet seam is used for any fabric that has a pile. A hairline seam is used on fine fabrics where a normal seam would show through and look untidy.

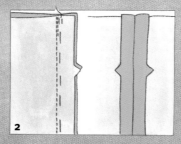

Flat seam

The flat seam is used to join fabrics of normal weight. To make a flat seam, follow the basic instructions for Constructing a seam (left).

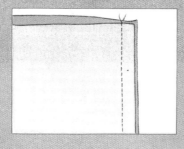

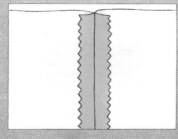

French seam

The french seam is a narrow seam, which encloses the raw edges of the fabric. It is used on fabrics which fray easily, such as fine, semi-transparent fabric. Do not use this seam on heavy fabrics, as the result will be bulky. The finished seam should be no wider than 5mm (¼ in). It is always pressed to one side.

1. Place the two pieces of fabric with the wrong sides facing. Pin, tack, and stitch about 1cm (⅜ in) from the raw edges. Trim both the seam allowances to 3mm (⅛ in).
2. Refold so the right sides are together and the seam is at the edge. Pin, tack and stitch along the seam again, this time 5mm (¼ in) from the edge.

Narrow finish seam

The narrow finish seam is used only on lightweight or semi-transparent fabrics. It is an inconspicuous way of joining fine fabrics and can be finished either by hand or by machine.

1. Place the two pieces of fabric together with the right sides facing. Pin, tack and stitch along the seamline. Remove all tacking stitches.

2. To finish by machine, trim the seam allowance to 5mm (¼ in) and zigzag over both.

3. To finish by hand, fold the seam allowances in to meet each other, as shown. Tack the folds together, press and slip stitch neatly. Remove all tacking.

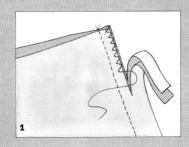

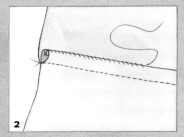

Seams for vinyl and leather

To ensure that puncture marks from pins do not spoil your finished bag, pin or tack only in the seam allowance or hold the edges together with paper clips. Use a specially coated presser foot on your machine to stop the fabric from sticking when it is stitched. Use wedge-shaped needles and change them frequently. Flatten seams open with a mallet.

Seaming pile fabrics

Stitch seams in the direction of the pile. Care must be taken to exert the correct amount of pressure on the fabric while stitching. The longer and denser the pile, the greater the need to reduce bulk from the seams.

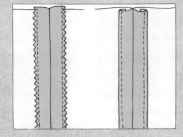

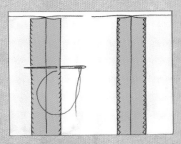

Finishing a seam

Seams can be finished by hand stitching the edges using overcast stitches, or by cutting along the seam allowance with pinking shears, as shown above.

fastenings

Zips, buttons and bows—whatever fastening you choose, make sure it is appropriate for the fabric and the purpose for which you intend to use the bag you are making. Fastenings are not just a way of securing your bag; they can also be made into a decorative feature and add a professional finish.

Creative clasps

Any bag—especially smart day bags or glitzy evening bags—will benefit from the addition of a unique clasp. Look out for beads, glass balls, coloured studs and ornate buttons taken from old bags discovered at the bottom of your wardrobe or in car boot sales. Glass diamanté clasps and tassels will add sparkle and glamour to evening bags. For a contemporary look, be creative with plastic or rubber tubing and shiny metal chains.

Buttons

Although they come in a huge variety of shapes, sizes and materials, buttons are made in basically two types—shank and sew-through. The shank has a solid top, with a shank beneath to accommodate thicker fabrics and prevent the button from pressing too hard against the buttonhole. You can also buy button blanks to cover in matching or contrasting fabrics.

Sew-through buttons have either two or four holes through which the button is sewn on. A zigzag sewing machine can be used to sew on these buttons.

Stitch the thread over a toothpick, to add 'give', then wind the thread at the base.

Use a button foot to machine on a button, adding a toothpick between fabric and button for 'give'.

Tips
- A four-hole button may have to be sewn with two separate stitchings.
- A button foot is included in some machine accessory boxes.
- Use contrasting coloured thread to sew on buttons.

Zips

There are three basic types of zip —conventional, open-ended and invisible. For most bags you would use the open-ended variety.

An open-ended zip should be inserted before any facings or hems are started. Use the zip foot on your machine to insert the zip or, if you are sewing by hand, use a half back stitch and double thread for strength.

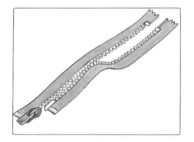

An open-ended zip is the most practical choice when making a bag.

Tips

- Before any zip is sewn in, the seam should be semi-finished and then tacked open.
- Match the colour of your zip to the fabric you are using, or use one a shade darker.
- Always match the zip length to the size of the opening.

Zips are made in many different weights and sizes, and whether you use metal or nylon is a matter of personal preference as both are of equal strength. Nylon zips are usually lighter in weight and more flexible than metal, and are available in a wider variety of colours. But you may choose a colourful chunky zip and make it into a feature of your bag.

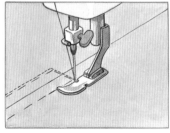

The easiest way to insert a zip is to place it in the centre of an open seam, with an equal amount of fabric on each side.

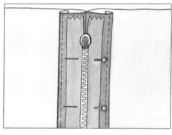

Pin the zip in position with the teeth over the seam opening. Tack 5mm (¼ in) in from the zip and remove the pins.

Using a zip foot, stitch close to the tacking line. Begin at the top of one side and work around the zip. Remove the tacking.

The bags

Start with embellishing a shop-bought bag, learn how to make basic bag shapes and graduate to creating a leather-fringed fake fur shoulderbag from scratch. These designs cover the full range of styles and materials – both traditional and contemporary – just right for any outfit.

*i*t takes just a couple of minutes to alter the appearance of a shop-bought bag and make it one-of-a-kind. All you need to do is add a favourite brooch, a corsage, braids and ribbons. Keep the bag shape and fabric as classic as possible, and you will find that you can use the same bag over and over again, in a multitude of ways.

shades
of grey

MATERIALS AND EQUIPMENT

- Shop-bought satin evening bag
- 50cm (20 in) beaded ribbon
- 50cm (20 in) fringed wool braid
- Artificial silk flower
- Favourite brooch
- Matching threads
- Scissors

1 FLOWER
Bend the stem of the artificial flower around the bow on the bag. Stitch into place using a fine needle.

1 BRAIDING
Measure the width of the decorative arc on the bag. Take twice the amount of beaded ribbon and fold the ends to the centre.

2 Stitch the ends of the ribbon in place to secure.

3 Place the ribbon over the arc and stitch carefully to the top and sides of the arc.

4 Take a piece of fringed wool braid. Wind it up into a ball, stitching the base as you go, until you get to the size of pom-pom you require.

5 At the cut edge, turn over 1cm (⅜ in). Stitch to finish the pom-pom and attach it to the centre of the bag.

1 BROOCH
Pin the brooch to the bag to conceal the bow.

he bright style of this embellished raffia bag will add a ray of sunshine to any outfit. The simple embroidery stitches, sewn in different-coloured wool, and the fun pom-poms hide the fact that this bag began life as a kitchen plant-pot holder.

easter basket

MATERIALS AND EQUIPMENT

- Raffia plant-pot holder
- Green wool (1 skein)
- Orange wool (1 skein)
- Pale yellow wool (4 skeins)
- Red wool (1 skein)
- Wool needle
- 10 pieces of card, 8cm x 8cm (3 in x 3 in)
- 16 necklace beads
- Metal handbag handle
- Scissors

1 Take the raffia plant-pot holder and stem stitch the stems of the decorative flowers in green wool with a wool needle.

2 Using a straight stitch, embroider the petals in orange and red wool, working from the centre outwards. Using green and pale yellow wool, stitch the grass close to the base of the bag.

3 Using a straight stitch, make six-pointed stars in orange and red wool at random points around the bag.

4 To make each pom-pom, take two squares of card. Find the centre by drawing a line through each corner.

5 Using the compass draw one large circle, followed by one small circle. Cut out the two circles from the card.

6 Place the two pieces of card together and wind the wool around the card, until the inner circle is almost full. With a sharp pair of scissors, cut through at the outer edge, to fluff out the wool.

7 Carefully pull the two pieces of card apart to reveal the centre, and tie a piece of wool tightly around the centre to secure. Cut the card from the pom-pom.

8 Sew the pom-poms onto the centre of each flower.

9 Unscrew one end of the metal handle and thread on the necklace beads. Screw the end back on. Blanket stitch the handle to the top edge of the bag.

10 Blanket stitch some pale yellow wool around the top edge of the bag.

*r*evamp a worn-out linen bag with this quick and easy makeover. You won't even need a sewing machine -all you'll need is a little imagination. This witty take on the famous nursery rhyme, *Baa Baa Black Sheep*, shows how you can find inspiration in the most unlikely of places.

Sheep and cloud templates

three bags full

MATERIALS AND EQUIPMENT

- Old linen bag
- 95cm x 20cm (37 in x 7 in) stretch sheepskin fabric
- 31cm x 20cm (12 in x 7 in) white felt
- 7.5cm x 7.5cm (3 in x 3 in) black felt
- 10cm x 10cm (4 in x 4 in) light blue felt
- 50cm (20 in) Bondaweb
- White thread
- Red thread
- Eyelet punch
- Scissors

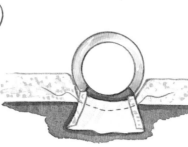

1 Measure around the base and top of the bag. Cut 2 sheepskin panels for the top, 1 panel for the bottom, and 2 panels to cover the base of the handles —all 10cm (4 in) wide.

2 With the right sides of the bag and the top sheepskin panels together, use running stitch to attach the panels along the top of the bag. Remember to turn in the end seams of the panels first. Using slip stitch, attach the sheepskin to the inside of the bag.

3 With right sides together, stitch on the handle panel to secure it to the bag.

4 Pull the sheepskin panel over the handle and slip stitch it to the inside of the bag.

5 Tack a line of red stitches around the bag, 5cm (2 in) from the base.

6 With right sides together, stitch the sheepskin panel around the base of the bag in line with the red stitches. Stitch together the side seam.

7 Fold under the seam allowance and slip stitch the sheepskin fabric to the base of the bag.

8 Iron Bondaweb to the back of the white, black and blue felt. Draw and cut out white sheep, black heads, and white and blue clouds onto the Bondaweb. Peel the Bondaweb backing off the sheep shapes and clouds. Iron them onto the bag. Mark the sheep eyes with a punch (or sew eyes with white thread). Peel the backing off the heads and stick onto the sheep.

*y*ou have found a treasure of a bag in an antique shop or have inherited a bag from an elderly aunt. The clasp is beautiful, but the rest of the bag is in tatters. Don't lose heart and stuff the bag at the back of your wardrobe. You can easily deconstruct the bag and add your own touch.

MATERIALS AND EQUIPMENT

- 23cm (9 in) beaded fabric (standard width 90cm/36 in)
- 23cm (9 in) lining fabric (standard width 90cm/36 in)
- 90cm (36 in) cord
- Two large tassels
- Matching threads
- Brown paper
- Pencils
- Scissors
- Pins and needles
- Sticky tape

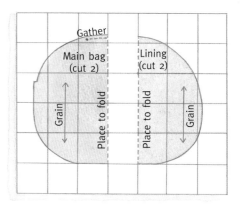

all that *glitters*

1 Cut the old bag fabric away from the clasp, leaving 5cm (2 in) of spare fabric still in the clasp.

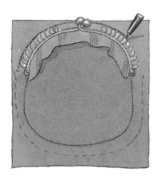

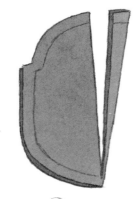

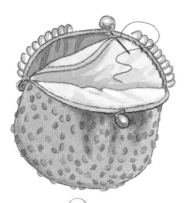

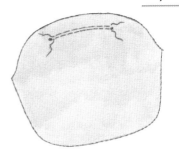

2 Place the clasp on brown paper, and draw around the edge. Decide on a given depth of fabric for your bag and draw on the brown paper, remembering to leave 2.5cm (1 in) for seam allowance.

3 Cut out the shape to make the pattern for your fabric. To add fullness to the bag, cut through the base line as shown and open up.

4 Pin the pattern onto a double layer of the beaded fabric and draw around it. Cut out two pieces of the main bag fabric.

5 Use a gathering stitch to gather between the dots shown on the pattern.

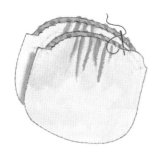

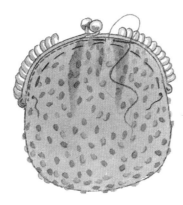

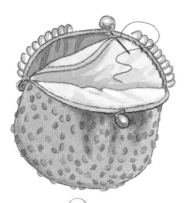

6 Turn down 1 cm (⅜ in) along the top edge of the bag and slip stitch the seam into place. With right sides together, stitch around the sides of the bag.

7 Attach the bag fabric to the clasp with tacking and a back stitch.

8 Using the main bag pattern, cut out the lining. Machine stitch the side seams. Turn under the allowance around the top edge and slip stitch the lining into the bag.

9 Attach the cord to the bag, securing the ends to the inside of the bag with a catch stitch. Sew the tassels onto the ends of the clasp.

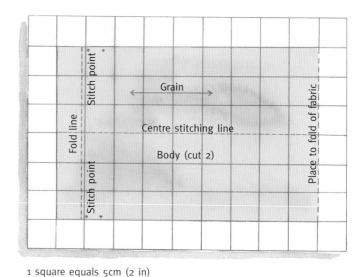

1 square equals 5cm (2 in)

*t*ough and colourful, this fabric was originally marketed as kite material. Yet it is perfect for a sporty backpack. If you add a fluorescent stripe down the middle, as shown here, the user of this bag will be easy to spot in the dark. Increase or decrease the measurements to make the bag as roomy as you wish.

sporty sack

MATERIALS AND EQUIPMENT

- 40cm (16 in) of pink rayon (standard width 90cm/36 in)
- 40cm (16 in) yellow rayon (standard width 90cm/36 in)
- 1m (3 ft) fluorescent tape
- 1.5m (5 ft) pink cord
- 1.5m (5 ft) yellow cord
- Matching thread
- Scissors

1 Use the pattern to cut out the main bag—once in the pink fabric and once in the yellow fabric—adding 2.5cm (1 in) for the seams.

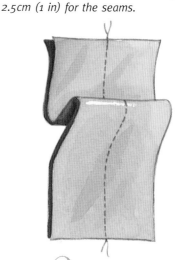

2 Place the two pieces of kite fabric together. Tack and stitch straight through the centre. Remove the tacking stitches.

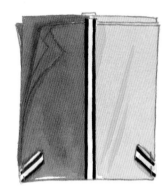

3 Open out the fabric. Tack and stitch the fluorescent tape in place over the central seam. Remove tacking stitches.

4 Fold the bag upwards with the right sides together. Use a cool iron to press the sides lightly together at the base.

5 Fold some fluorescent tape in half to form a loop and cut at an angle. Repeat.

6 Position the loops of tape at the base of the bag, and tack into place.

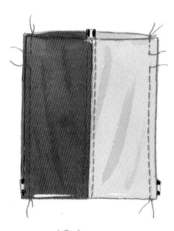

7 Machine the side seams, leaving a gap for the drawstring. Turn the bag through to the right side and take out the tacks.

8 Fold the bag over at the top. Machine a double row of stitches in contrasting thread at the top edge.

9 Feed the cord through one base loop and through the top casing, and knot at the base loop. Repeat with some contrasting cord for the other side of the bag.

- 30cm (12 in) quilted silk (standard width 36 in/90cm)
- 30cm (12 in) black lining (standard width 36 in/90cm)
- 30cm (12 in) iron-on interfacing (standard width 36 in/90cm)
- Corrugated plastic card
- Two tassels
- 1.5m (5 ft) cord (optional)
- Matching thread
- Scissors
- Craft knife
- Cutting board

*R*eminiscent of an Edwardian-style smoking jacket this elegant evening purse is deceptively simple to make, yet utterly sophisticated. The basic shape can be tailored to suit your outfit. Here, the fabric is an offcut of pre-quilted silk, jazzed up with antique black tassels – perfect for that little black number. However, taffetta, velvet, organza silk or beaded fabric would work equally well.

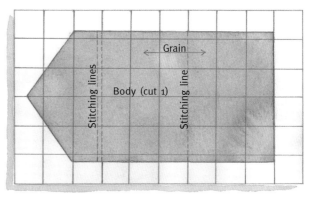

1 square equals 5cm (2 in)

tantalising tassels

1 Use the pattern to cut out the main purse fabric, adding 2.5cm (1 in) for the seams. Cut the lining to the same measurements.

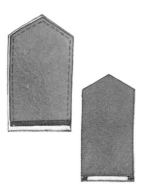

2 Cut out a piece of lightweight iron-on interfacing to the same main pattern and iron it to the wrong side of the fabric.

3 On the lining, sew a small hem at the bottom of the fabric.

4 Keeping the right sides together, tack and stitch the lining and fabric together. Turn through to the right side and press. Remove the tacking stitches.

5 Using the pattern, cut out two pieces of corrugated card.

6 Slot one piece of card into the top section, pushing through to the top. If the fabric is too tight, trim the card to fit snugly. Using a piping foot, machine a line of stitching to hold the card in place.

7 Machine stitch a second line 2.5cm (1 in) away from the last stitching line. Insert the second piece of card, and use the piping foot to machine stitch a line below the card, fixing it into position.

8 Turn over the seam allowance of the bottom edge of the fabric and stitch the lining down using a slip stitch.

9 Fold the bottom section over the middle section and tack both sides in place. Machine a line of stitches down both sides. Stitch two decorative tassels to the inside of the bag. Add an optional piece of cord for a shoulder bag.

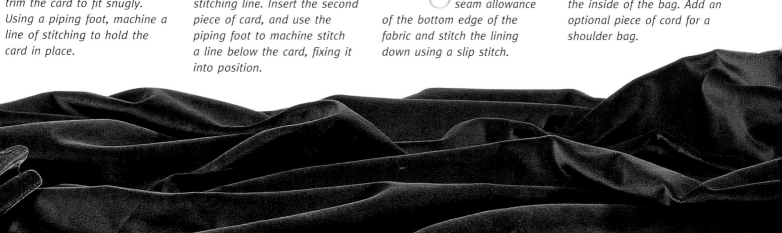

*b*ridesmaids are easy to overlook when it comes to accessories, but providing them with tailor-made bags can make all the difference. Using beautiful fabric that complements your wedding scheme, add pretty beading and velvet and they'll no doubt want to use them again. If you have any fabric left over, make matching handkerchiefs—they'll come in handy on the Big Day!

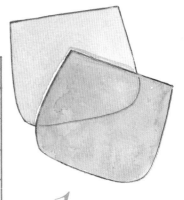

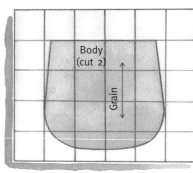

Body (cut 2)

Grain

1 square equals 5cm (2 in)

1 Use the pattern measurements to cut out the back and front of the main bag—in the silk fabric, the organza, and the lining fabric—adding an extra 2.5cm (1 in) for the seams.

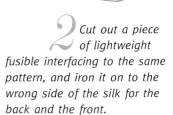

2 Cut out a piece of lightweight fusible interfacing to the same pattern, and iron it on to the wrong side of the silk for the back and the front.

wedding belles

MATERIALS AND EQUIPMENT

- 30cm (12 in) pink paper taffeta (standard width 90cm/36 in)
- 30cm (12 in) printed organza (standard width 90cm/36 in)
- 30cm (12 in) lining fabric (standard width 90cm/36 in)
- 30cm (12 in) fusible (iron-on) interfacing
- 40 cm (16 in) bead fringing
- 40 cm (16 in) velvet ribbon
- Matching thread

3 Tack the organza pieces to the right side of the silk for the back and the front. Pin and tack some beaded fringing to the bag as shown.

4 Position some velvet ribbon over the top edge of the beading. Tack the top and bottom of the ribbon to the bag.

5 Keeping the right sides together, tack and stitch the sides and base of the bag, taking care not to trap the beads in the side seam. Trim seam allowance to 5mm (¼ in).

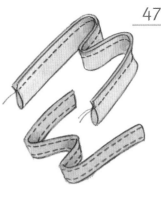

6 To make the handles, cut two strips of silk and organza 30cm x 4cm (12 in x 1½ in). With the right sides together, fold them in half lengthways. Machine stitch down the long edge. Trim the seam to 5mm (¼ in).

7 Turn the bag through to the right side. Press with a cool iron. Using a machine, topstitch along both lengths of material close to the edge, and topstitch again close to the previous line of stitching. Place the handles to the right side of the bag and tack to secure them.

8 Tack and stitch along the seams of the lining fabric, leaving an opening at the bottom as shown above. Trim and press.

9 Slip the lining over the bag with the right sides facing. Tack along the top edge, just above the top of the ribbon edge. Machine stitch in place. Remove tacking stitches.

10 Turn in the lining seam, and stitch. Slip the lining back into the bag. Tack along the edges of the ribbon to secure the lining, beads and ribbon. Machine stitch to finish.

MATERIALS AND EQUIPMENT

- 30cm (12 in) purple slubbed silk (standard width 90cm/36 in)
- 30cm (12 in) gold pleated metallic organza (standard width 90cm/36 in)
- 20cm (8 in) gold lining fabric (standard width 90cm/36 in)
- 1m (40 in) gold cord
- 4 large purple glass or plastic teardrop beads
- 12 medium bronze beads
- Pot of small bronze glass embroidery beads
- Matching threads
- Sticky tape

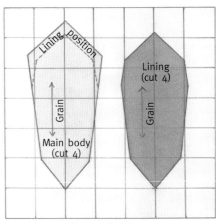

Lining position

Lining (cut 4)

Grain

Main body (cut 4)

Grain

1 square equals 5cm (2 in)

1 Using the pattern, cut out four pieces of gold fabric for the main body of the bag, four purple shapes for the purple panels and four pieces of lining fabric adding an extra 2.5cm (1 in) for the seams.

*a*t first glance, the pattern for this opera bag looks unusual, but it makes a wonderful teardrop shape, mirrored by the purple teardrop beads. Take your pattern to the shop with you, so that the fabric can be cut in the most economical way.

drama queen

2 Pin and tack the organza to the gold lining on all four pieces, with the wrong side of the organza to the right side of the gold fabric.

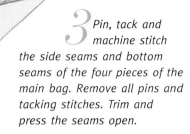

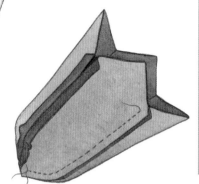

3 Pin, tack and machine stitch the side seams and bottom seams of the four pieces of the main bag. Remove all pins and tacking stitches. Trim and press the seams open.

4 Turn over the top edge of organza, mitering the corners at the peak of the corner.

5 To make the purple lining, pin, tack and machine stitch the purple silk panels to 12mm (½ in) from the top edge. Remove all pins and tacking stitches. Trim and press the seams open.

6 Cut the gold cord in half. Place the ends of the cord to the inside of the bag. Catch stitch the cords into place.

Tip Before cutting the cord, wrap some sticky tape around the area to be cut, to prevent the cord from fraying.

7 Slip the lining into the bag, with the wrong sides matching. Turn under the top edge and slip stitch the lining to the main bag.

8 Add 10cm (4 in) of small bronze embroidery beads onto bronze-coloured thread. Using a separate needle and thread, catch stitch the line of beads onto the edge of the purple panels at every fifth bead. Repeat this until all the purple edges have been piped.

9 To finish, string a purple drop bead then three copper beads onto some thread and stitch to the bag at each seam point.

*t*he perfect accessory for a racing event or a summer picnic, this bold bag makes a witty statement. The novelty turf is available already made up from garden centres and novelty shops, but you can add your own personal touch, such as a fluttering butterfly or two.

MATERIALS AND EQUIPMENT

- 1 square patch of novelty turf (including flowers) 25cm x 25cm (10 in by 10 in)
- 25cm (10 in) silk lining (standard width 90cm/36 in)
- 2 decorative butterflies (on wire)
- 6m (20 ft) of green satin ribbon
- 35cm (14 in) of transparent tubing (from a hardware shop)
- Leather punch
- Matching thread

green pastures

1 Bind the top and bottom edges of the novelty turf with green ribbon. Knot and stitch the ends to hold them in place.

2 Fold the turf in half, and bind the sides together. Knot and stitch the ends to hold them in place.

3 Using the leather punch, make a hole at the end of each tube.

4 Stitch the transparent tubing to the top of the bag.

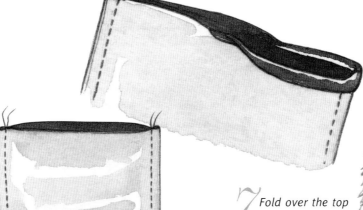

5 Bind the butterflies to the turf square, using the attached wire.

6 Cut 25cm x 25cm (10 in x 10 in) square of lining fabric. Fold in half and stitch up the sides with a French seam.

7 Fold over the top edge and stitch a double hem.

8 Push the lining into the bag and slip stitch along the top edge.

*e*xpress yourself with a feather boa and fancy brooch. Keep your outfit simple and you can really push the boat out with your accessories. The materials used for this stylish bag are simple and economical, but the overall effect is luxurious and one-of-a-kind.

feathered friend

MATERIALS AND EQUIPMENT

- Hardback book the size of bag you intend to make
- Galvanised wire 28cm x 30cm (11 in x 12 in) from a hardware shop
- Thin black feather boa 28cm (11 in) long
- 28cm (11 in) purple organza lining (standard width 90cm/36 in)
- 50cm (20 in) rubber tubing (from bicycle shop)
- 2 butterfly catches
- Leather punch
- Fine wire gauge 24 (0.5mm)
- Pliers
- Metal file
- Wire cutters
- Matching thread
- Optional brooch

1 Following the pattern, cut the galvanised wire into three pieces with pliers.

Main body (cut 1)

Grain

Side (cut 2)

1 square equals 5cm (2 in)

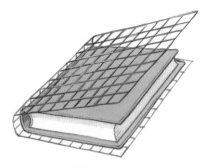

2 Fold the large piece of galvanised wire over the book to make a 'U' shape.

Tip Make sure your book is not larger than the wire.

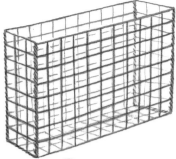

3 Attach the two side pieces to the main bag with galvanised wire, oversewing the pieces together. Wear away any sharp edges with a metal file.

4 Make a hole at both ends of the rubber tubing with a leather punch. Place the handle ends to the outside of the bag, and secure them in place with butterfly catches.

5 Using the pattern, cut out the lining fabric, adding 2.5cm (1 in) for the seams. Machine stitch the side seams and the base line. Trim and neaten the seam allowance, using a zigzag stitch on your machine.

6 Turn the top edge of the lining by 1 cm (³⁄₈ inch) and tack it into place. Using matching thread, oversew the lining to the top edge of the bag along the folded edge.

7 Cut the boa to fit the top of the bag. Stitch the ends together and bind with thread. Stitch the boa to the organza at 2.5cm (1 in) intervals. To finish, add a favourite brooch.

*t*here's something
flirty and French about the style of this bag, but the materials are deceptively down-to-earth. Grey wire mesh and grey rubber cord, available from a hardware shop, are the basic ingredients, lifted by bright red rosebuds and an artificial rose.

red, red rose

MATERIALS AND EQUIPMENT

- Piece of 50cm x 20cm (20 in x 8 in) galvanised grey wire
- Piece of 6cm x 23cm (2.5 in x 9 in) grey wire mesh
- 20 rosebuds
- 1 artificial rose
- 20cm (8 in) organza lining (standard width 90cm/36 in)
- 1m (40 in) silver raffia braid
- 1.5m (60 in) grey rubber cord (available from a craft shop)
- 0.5mm (gauge 24) grey fine wire
- Small piece of red ribbon

1 Cut out two pieces of galvanised wire from the pattern.

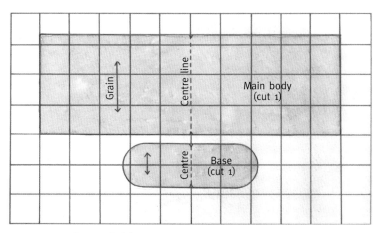

Grain

Centre line

Main body
(cut 1)

Centre

Base
(cut 1)

1 square equals 5cm (2 in)

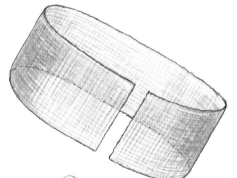

2 *Bend the larger piece of galvanised wire into an oval shape.*

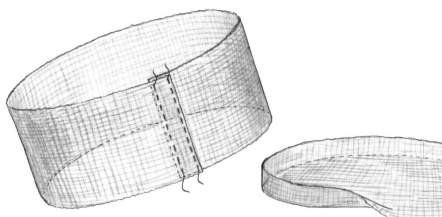

3 *Overlap the back join by 12mm (½ in) and stitch together the two ends with grey wire. Turn up the bottom edge by 1cm (⅜ in).*

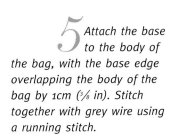

5 *Attach the base to the body of the bag, with the base edge overlapping the body of the bag by 1cm (⅜ in). Stitch together with grey wire using a running stitch.*

4 *Take the smaller piece of mesh and turn up the edge by 1cm (⅜ in).*

6 *Decorate the bag with the rosebuds and an artificial rose. Pin and stitch in place using grey wire. Tie the red ribbon in a bow around the rose stem.*

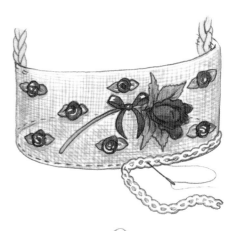

7 Cut the rubber cord into three pieces and plait to form the handle.

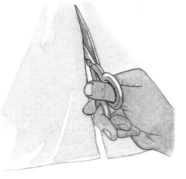

8 Turn the top edge of the main bag in by 1cm (⅜ in). Stitch the handles using grey wire to the inside of the side seams.

9 Before lining the bag, stitch the raffia braid with grey wire onto the bottom edge.

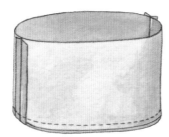

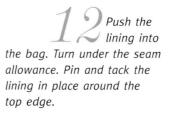

12 Push the lining into the bag. Turn under the seam allowance. Pin and tack the lining in place around the top edge.

10 Cut a piece of organza 50cm x 20cm (20 in x 8 in) to make up a lining.

11 Stitch the two short edges of the lining to form the seam. Trim and press open. Attach the base of the lining to the main body. Trim the seam and press open.

13 On the right side of the bag, pin on the raffia braiding. Use a running stitch to attach the lining and braid simultaneously to the main bag. Remove all pins and tacking stitches.

*i*nspired by a favourite tribal necklace and offcuts of ethnic fabric found on holiday, this bag was designed as a sentimental tribute to fond memories in the sun. The bright bag is reinforced with suede corners to give it extra strength. Make sure in advance that your necklace is robust enough to be used as a handle.

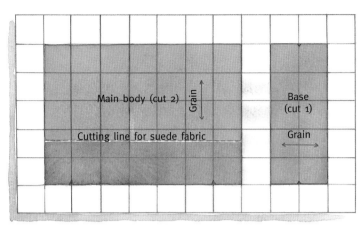

Main body (cut 2)   Grain

Cutting line for suede fabric

Base (cut 1)

Grain

1 square equals 5cm (2 in)

ethnic *chic*

MATERIALS AND EQUIPMENT

- 30cm (12 in) yellow printed fabric (standard width 90cm/36 in)
- 30cm (12 in) matching lining (standard width 90cm/36 in)
- 30cm (12 in) heavy iron-on interfacing (standard width 90cm/36 in)
- 2 pieces of 36cm x 10cm (14 in x 4 in) suede (width 90cm/36 in)
- Beaded necklace
- 2 magnetic fasteners
- Matching thread
- Pinking shears
- Scissors

1 Use the pattern measurements to cut out the fabric for the back and front of the main bag, adding 2.5cm (1 in) for the seams. Cut out the suede panels, using pinking shears on one edge only. Cut some interfacing using the pattern and iron it onto the wrong side of the main fabric.

2 Place one suede panel onto the right side of the main fabric with the non-pinked edge along the bottom edge. Tack and machine a double row of stitches along the pinked edge. Remove the tacking stitches.

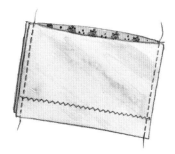

3 Keeping the right sides together, stitch the side seams of the main fabric. Trim and press the seams open.

4 Cut out the fabric and two layers of interfacing for the base, adding 2.5cm (1 in) for the seam. Iron two layers of interfacing onto the wrong side of the fabric.

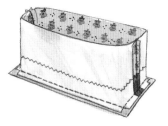

5 Turn the main body of the bag inside out. With right sides together, tack and stitch the base to the bag. Snip into the corner, trim excess fabric off seams and remove tacking.

6 Turn the bag through to the right side. To insert the magnetic fasteners, first mark their position on the fabric. Make small incisions where the fasteners are to be attached, and push them through.

7 Fold over the top edge of the bag, tack along the top edge 2.5cm (1 in) from the edge, and stitch along the tacking line. Remove the tacking stitches.

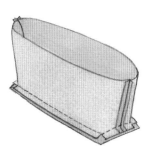

8 Make up the lining.Use the measurements on the pattern, but just 2mm (¹/₁₂ in) smaller. Place the lining onto the inside of the bag, and attach it to the bag using a slip stitch.

9 Stitch the ends of the necklace securely into the inside of the side seams.

*t*his stylish fake fur and velvet shoulder bag will remind you of warm, winter mufflers on the coldest of days. Reusing a thin patent leather belt for the shoulder strap is a witty touch, but you could use thick leather cord instead. By keeping the bag fairly simple, the different textures of the piece are the main attraction.

winter warmer

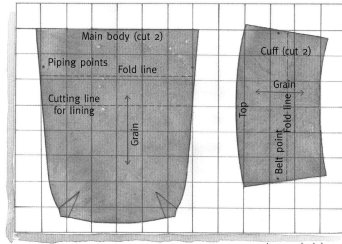

Main body (cut 2)

Piping points

Fold line

Cutting line for lining

Grain

Cuff (cut 2)

Grain

Top

Belt point

Fold line

1 square equals 5cm (2 in)

MATERIALS AND EQUIPMENT

- 50cm (20 in) black velvet (standard width 90cm/36 in)
- 20cm (8 in) fur fabric (standard width 90cm/36 in)
- 60cm (24 in) black leather piping
- Patent leather belt (large)
- 30cm (12 in) lining fabric (standard width 90cm/36 in)
- Iron-on interfacing
- Matching thread
- Ruler or tape measure
- Scissors

1 Use the pattern to cut out the back and front of the main bag from the velvet fabric, adding an extra 2.5cm (1 in) for the seams.

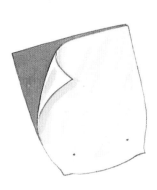

2 Cut out a piece of lightweight iron-on interfacing to the same main bag pattern and iron it to the wrong side of the velvet.

3 Tack and machine stitch the darts on the back and front of the bag. To reduce bulkiness, press the darts of one piece towards the outer seam and the darts of the other piece towards the centre.

4 On one piece of velvet, tack on the leather piping to the wrong side. Fan the piping outwards at the top, so that it is hidden in the seam when the fabric is turned the right way around.

5 Place the right sides of the two main pieces of material together and tack. Machine stitch along the previous tacking line, using a piping foot, from the top of one side to the top of the other. Remove all tacking stitches and trim the seam allowance to 5mm (¼ in).

6 Cut out the fake fur fabric to the cuff template, adding an extra 2.5cm (1 in) for the seams.

Tip *If you machine stitch a fake fur fabric, use a larger stitch on the machine. When complete, using a pin, tease out the threads on the right side and secure.*

7 Keeping right sides together, pin and whipstitch down both side seams of the facing, leaving a small opening for the handles.

8 Turn the cuff through to the right side and attach to the top of the velvet bag, tacking along the top edge. Using a large stitch, machine around the entire top edge of the bag. Trim to 1cm ³⁄₈ in, remove tacking stitches, and turn through to the right side. Turn the cuff over onto the bag.

9 Cut the belt in half. Punch a hole at each end. Put each end through the openings on the sides. Stitch the ends to the bag's seam. To secure the cuff, stitch through the facing seam. Cross-stitch the bottom of the cuff to the interfacing.

10 Cut out the lining following instructions on the pattern. Tack and stitch the darts, and hand stitch the lining into the bag. Remove all tacking stitches.

*t*here's no limit to the creative force you can unleash when making your own bags. Go freestyle with the odds and ends of earrings, brooches and beads sitting at the back of your jewellery box. They're just going to waste at the moment, so it's time for some stylish recycling.

MATERIALS AND EQUIPMENT

- Spool of brass wire, 1.6mm (gauge 14)
- 40cm x 50cm (16 in x 20 in) offcut of toning organza
- Beads, buttons, earrings, brooches, odd bits of necklaces
- Fine wire, 0.3mm (gauge 28)
- Matching thread
- Wire cutters
- Small pliers
- Adhesive

gilded cage

1 Using the small pliers, bend the brass wire into loops and circles, making two oval shapes about 20cm x 16cm (8 in x 6 in).

2 Make a long strip 35cm x 5cm (14 in x 2 in) to form the base and side panels, looping and bending the wire to your liking using the pliers.

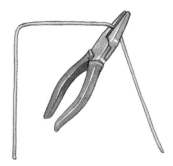

3 To make the handles, bend the brass wire into a three-sided square using the pliers.

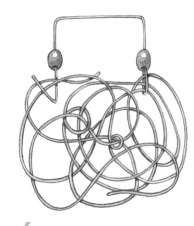

4 Slip two large beads onto the handles and fold up the ends with the pliers. Attach the handles to the main bag. Then slip the beads back over the ends of the wire and glue into place.

5 Join all three pieces together with the fine wire.

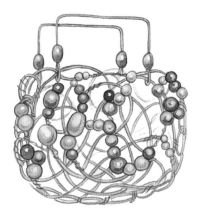

6 Thread beads, baubles and anything else you have hiding in your treasure box, onto the fine wire and twist it around the brass wire loops, knotting the ends.

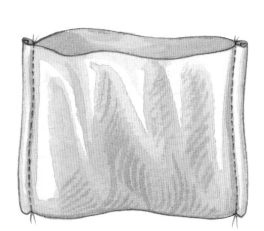

7 Fold the lining fabric in half. Tack and machine stitch the side seams together, using a French seam. Push the lining into the bag.

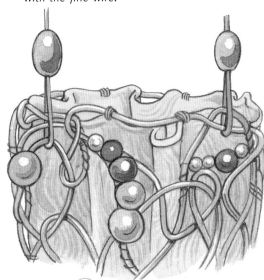

8 Turn over a double hem at the top edge of the lining and hand stitch. Using the wire, gather the top of the lining as you stitch it to the brass wire.

Wool makes a warm, cozy and flexible bag material, and is easy to use, even if you are a beginner at knitting. Personalise your bag with decorative mirrors for an Asian feel, or use decorative embroidery stitches in contrasting thread.

MATERIALS AND EQUIPMENT

- 2 knitting needles, size 7 or 8
- Poodle or bouclé yarn
- Approximately 60 small Indian decorative mirrors
- 1 large Indian decorative mirror
- 30cm (12 in) matching lining (standard width 90cm/36 in)
- Matching thread
- Scissors
- One large, flat button, the same size as the large mirror

mirror, mirror

1 Cast on enough stitches, depending on your wool, to make a 30cm (12 in) wide piece of fabric.

2 Knit one, purl one to a length of 65cm (26 in). Cast off.

3 With the right sides together, fold up and whip stitch the side seams using the wool.

4 Cast on stitches to make the handle, 6cm (2½ in) wide. Knit one, purl one to a length of 81cm (32 in) and cast off. Use some wool to hand stitch the handle onto the side seams of the main bag.

5 To make the looped fastener, cast on stitches equivalent to 2cm (¾ in) wide. Knit one, purl one to a length of 30cm (12 in). Attach the loop to the right side of the bag with wool.

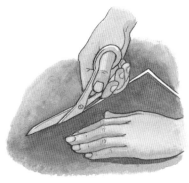

6 Catch stitch the decorative mirrors onto the back and front of the bag.

7 Glue the large decorative mirror onto a large button and stitch into position as a catch for the loop fastener.

8 Cut the lining fabric to 30cm x 65cm (12 in x 26 in). Tack and machine stitch the side seams, trim and press them open.

9 Turn over the top edge by 1cm (⅜ in). Push the lining into the bag and slip stitch the top edge into place.

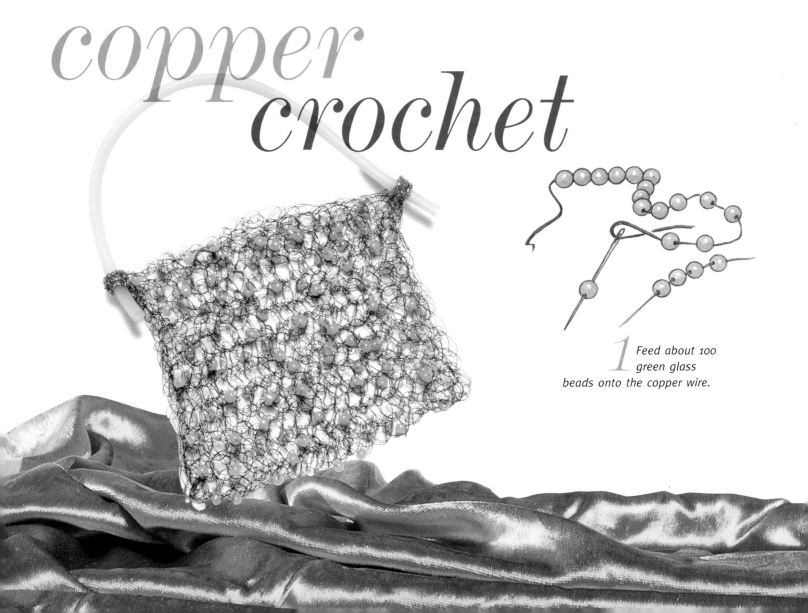

*C*rochet need not be limited to yarn or string... why not create a copper wire and green glass bead bag to stand out from the crowd? The technique is so simple and the materials long-lasting that you won't be able to keep this design to yourself for long.

MATERIALS AND EQUIPMENT

- No. 6 crochet hook
- 100 green glass beads
- 0.3mm (gauge 28) diameter copper craft wire
- 30cm (12 in) green rubber tubing
- 60 small copper coloured glass embroidery beads

copper
crochet

1 Feed about 100 green glass beads onto the copper wire.

2 Push the green beads down the copper wire and cast on 20 stitches using a No. 6 crochet needle.

3 Begin to crochet. Add one bead into every second stitch on every second row (so that the beads appear in alternate spaces). Crochet to a length of 50cm (20 in).

4 Fold the crocheted piece in half and whip stitch the side seams using copper wire.

5 Stitch the tubing to the outside of the side seams with a needle and wire.

6 Feed about 30 small copper beads onto the remaining wire. Wrap the beaded wire around the tubing to hide the stitches, and knot to finish.

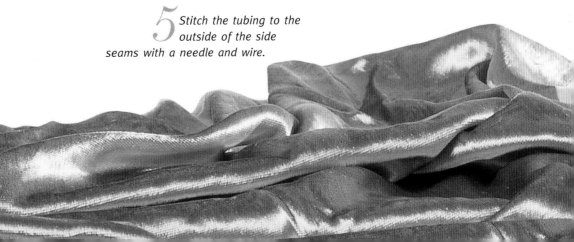

MATERIALS AND EQUIPMENT

- 30cm (12 in) jade silk (standard width 90cm/36 in)
- 30cm x 4cm (12 in x 1½ in) jade silk
- 30cm (12 in) wadding interlining (standard width 90cm/36 in)
- 30cm (12 in) Vylene (standard width 90cm/36 in)
- 30cm (12 in) lining (standard width 90cm/36 in)
- Matching thread
- Scissors
- Matching thread

S haped like a corset worn in a Parisian chorus line, this jade green evening bag is made even more sumptuous with a rose corsage created from complementary shades of green organza ribbon. The delicate silk of the bag is strengthened with wadding interlining, and the whole piece is given a lift with some simple quilting.

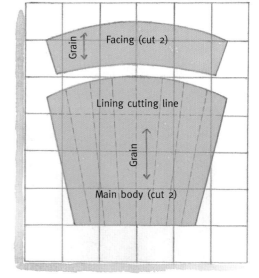

Facing (cut 2)

Grain

Lining cutting line

Grain

Main body (cut 2)

1 square equals 5cm (2 in)

french fancy

1 Use the pattern to cut out the silk fabric for the back and front of the main bag, adding 2.5cm (1 in) for the seams. Cut out the Vylene for the back of the bag only, using the same pattern.

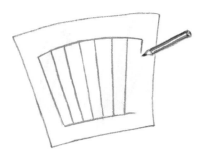

2 Cut out the Vylene and wadding for the front of the bag using the pattern, adding 2.5cm (1 in) for the seams. Use the template to mark up the quilting lines on the Vylene.

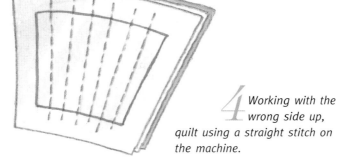

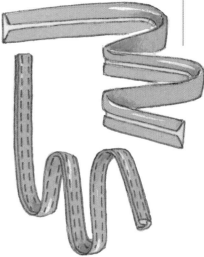

4 Working with the wrong side up, quilt using a straight stitch on the machine.

3 Sandwich the wadding between the silk and the Vylene. Tack all the way round, and also through the centre.

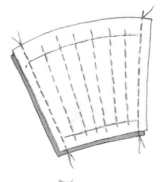

5 Keeping the right sides together, place the back and the front together. Tack and stitch them into place. Trim the seam allowance.

6 Make the straps by folding the long edges of a strip of fabric 40cm (16 in) long by 4cm (1½ in) wide to the centre. Fold the long edges into the centre once more. Tack and machine stitch along the edges. Repeat this to make four straps.

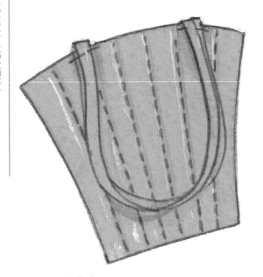

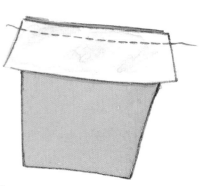

8 Cut some facing fabric and
iron-on interfacing using the
pattern. Iron these together. Cut out the lining
fabric from the pattern, adding 2.5cm (1 in)
for the seams.

9 Machine stitch
the facing to the
lining, keeping the right sides
together. Trim and press open.

7 Pair the straps,
two by two, and
tack into position at the top
edge of the bag by the second
row of quilting.

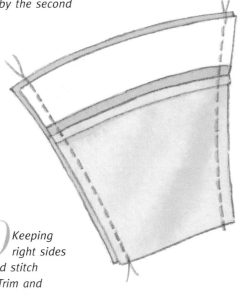

11 With the right sides
together, place the
lining over the bag. Tack and stitch into
place around top edge. Trim, and turn
the lining through to the inside of the
bag. Remove tacking stitches.

10 Keeping
right sides
together, tack and stitch
the side seams. Trim and
press open. Remove the
tacking stitches.

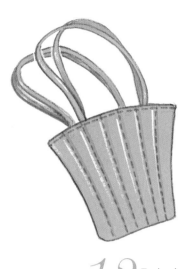

12 Tack along the top edge. Press, and machine two rows of stitching, close together, around the top edge of the bag.

13 Pull the lining back out of the bag. Turn under the seam allowance along the unstitched edge. Tack and stitch into place. Return the lining back into the bag.

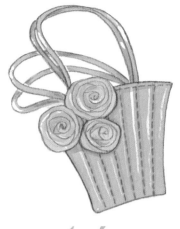

14 As an optional decorative feature, stitch on a corsage made from matching light and dark green organza ribbons.

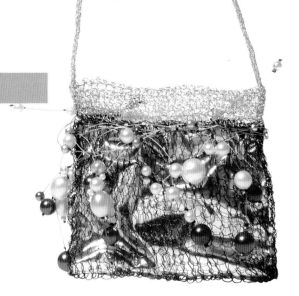

*i*nstead of relying on more traditional fabrics such as silk, satin or leather to make a bag, create your own evening bag from knitted wire and fake pearls. By using the spool-knitting technique learned in your childhood, you can quickly transform your bag into a unique piece of jewellery.

knit and pearl

MATERIALS AND EQUIPMENT

- 2 knitting needles (size 8)
- 0.3mm (gauge 28) diameter purple craft wire
- 0.3mm (gauge 28) diameter silver craft wire
- Old costume jewellery (fake pearls, brooch, earrings)
- 15cm (6 in) silver lamé lining (standard width 90cm/36 in)
- Wooden cotton spool
- 6 thumbtacks
- Hammer
- Crochet hook
- Matching threads

1 Cast on 25 stitches with the purple craft wire.

2 Knit one, purl one to a length of 50cm (20 in). Cast off.

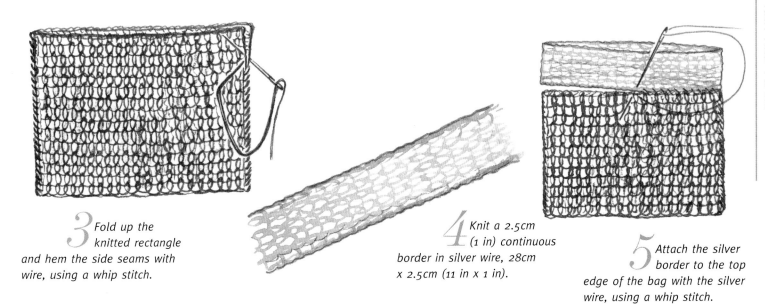

3 Fold up the knitted rectangle and hem the side seams with wire, using a whip stitch.

4 Knit a 2.5cm (1 in) continuous border in silver wire, 28cm x 2.5cm (11 in x 1 in).

5 Attach the silver border to the top edge of the bag with the silver wire, using a whip stitch.

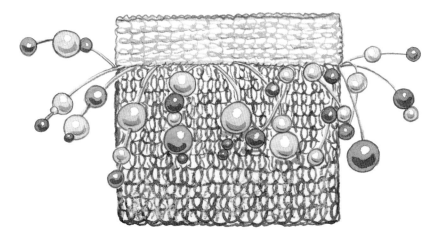

6 Decorate with pearls, beads, brooches and baubles of your choice.

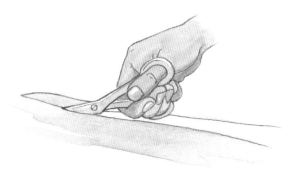

7 Cut out a piece of silver fabric, 14cm x 50cm (5½ x 20 in).

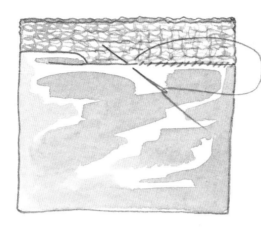

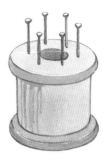

8 Fold the fabric in half and join the sides together with a French seam.

9 Turn over the top edge of the bag. Slip stitch the silver fabric to the cuff edge, as shown.

10 To make the handle of the bag, take a wooden cotton spool and hammer 6 thumbtacks into a circle around the hole.

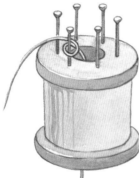

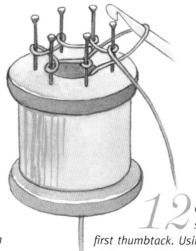

11 To spool knit, cast on by passing the silver wire around the front of a thumbtack, loop it around the back of the same tack, turning the loop in an anti-clockwise direction. Move in a clockwise direction to the next tack and wind the wire around all the thumbtacks.

12 Cast a second stitch onto the first thumbtack. Using a crochet hook, pick up and lift the lower of the two stitches and pass it over the top stitch. Drop this into the hole of the spool. Continue knitting until you have a strip 50cm (20 in) long.

13 To cast off, pick the stitches off the spool with a crochet hook. Secure by threading the ends of the wire into the loose stitches and knot.

14 Catch stitch the handle to the side seams of the bag, using the silver wire.

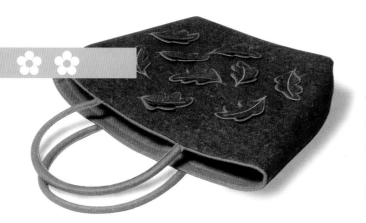

*r*emember being caught
in an autumn breeze
with the leaves swirling around your feet? The clever use
of cut-out leaf motifs gives this felt shopper a three-
dimensional edge that is bound to be a talking point.
Easy to use, felt is a hard-wearing alternative to silk, yet
looks just as appealing – perfect for trips to the shop.

falling
leaves

MATERIALS AND EQUIPMENT

- 40cm (16 in) brown felt
  (standard width 140cm/54 in)
- 10cm (4 in) orange felt
  (standard width 140cm/54 in)
- 40cm (16 in) lining (standard
  width 90cm/36 in)
- 2 small pieces of iron-on
  interfacing (standard width
  90cm/36 in)
- 1m (40 in) leather cord
- Matching thread
- Ruler or tape measure
- Scissors
- Craft knife
- Cutting board

Leaf template (at 50%)

1 square equals 5cm (2 in)

Facing
(cut 2)

Main body
(cut 2)

Place to fold of fabric

Grain

Place to fold

Grain

Base
(cut 1)

1 Using the pattern, cut out the body and the
base of the bag from brown felt. Cut out the
facing and 2 strips for the handles, 64cm x 5cm (25 in x
2 in), from the orange felt. Add an extra 2.5cm (1 in) for
the seams.

2 Cut out a piece of lightweight iron-on interfacing to the same main bag, handles and facing templates and iron them on to the wrong side of the fabric.

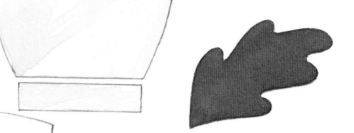

3 Using the leaf template, cut out 9 leaves in brown felt.

4 Cut a piece of light orange contrasting felt larger than the leaves. Machine a line of straight stitch through the centre of the leaves to hold the two pieces in place.

5 Using the brown leaf as a guide, trim the orange leaves about 5mm (¼ in) larger than the brown leaf.

6 Pin the leaves on to one side of the bag as illustrated. Tack and machine stitch them in place using a narrow zigzag stitch.

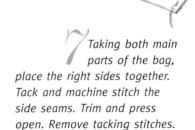

7 Taking both main parts of the bag, place the right sides together. Tack and machine stitch the side seams. Trim and press open. Remove tacking stitches.

8 On the right side, machine a double row of stitching.

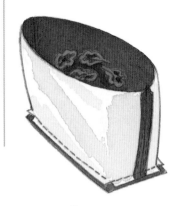

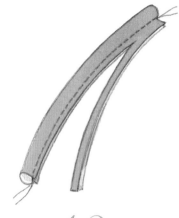

9 Pin, tack and machine stitch the base into the bag, keeping the right sides together. Snip into the corners.

10 Using the pattern, make up the lining as shown in steps 7, 8 and 9, but make it 2mm (¹⁄₁₂ in) smaller. Turn the bag through to the right side. Drop in the lining and tack around the outer edge.

11 Take the leather cord, and cut each end at an angle with a craft knife. Reinforce the ends of the felt handles with iron-on interfacing.

12 Wrap the orange felt around the leather cord and tack it into position. Using a piping foot, machine stitch as close to the cord as possible. Repeat the stitching to reinforce the seam. Trim the felt close to the stitch line. Remove tacking stitches.

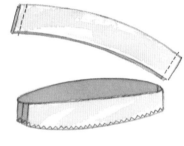

13 Place the handles to the right side of the bag.

14 Keeping the right sides together, machine stitch the side seams of the contrasting felt facing. Trim the seam allowance and press open. Neaten the lower edge with a row of zigzag stitching.

15 Attach the facing to the bag. Tack and stitch into position. Remove tacking stitches.

16 *Turn the facing over to the wrong side and tack through the seam allowance, so that the handles sit correctly. Stitch through the well of the seam line to keep the facing in place. Put another row of stitching 2.5cm (1 in) below this line.*

t his personalised patchwork bag can be made from a single piece of material or any leftover remnants found in the workbox. You can customise it further with decorative braid, ribbon, motifs, even sequins, buttons and beads. Here, the bag has been personalised with ribbon and braid bought in Nepal, and will serve as a useful souvenir of a happy trip.

patchwork perfect

MATERIALS AND EQUIPMENT

- 12 squares in all, 23cm x 23cm (9 in x 9 in), 6 different colours
- Strip of fabric 4.5 in (12cm) long
- 46cm (18 in) lining fabric
- 4.5m (5 yds) ribbon
- 4.5m (5 yds) fine braid
- matching thread
- 4 decorative motifs

Cuff (cut 2)

Cut 2

Cut 2

Cut 2

Grain

Main body (cut out x 2 in panels according to color)

Main body (cut out in panels x 2)

Cut 2

Cut 2

Cut 2

Base line

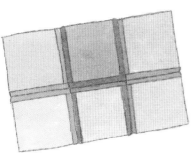

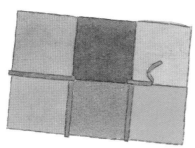

1 Sew the squares, right sides together, in 2 rows of 3 squares. Repeat for the back.

2 Disguise the seams of the patchwork with fine braid.

3 Attach the decorative ribbon to the central panel on the front and back.

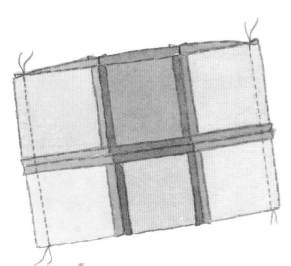

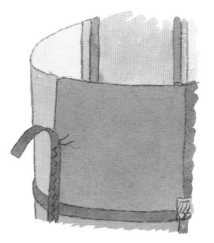

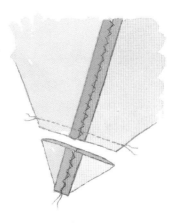

4 Tack and stitch together the right sides of the side seams. Trim and press open. Then tack and machine stitch the bottom seam. Remove all tacking stitches and turn right side out.

5 On the right side, machine the fine braid down the side seam using a zigzag stitch.

6 With the bag inside out, flatten the corner. Stitch across the corner and trim off the edge.

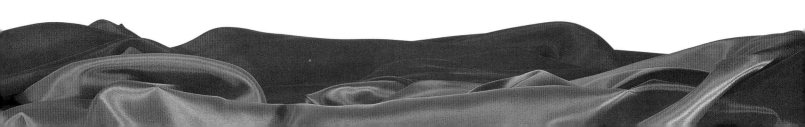

7 Take the fabric for the top panel and, with the right sides together, stitch the side seams. Trim the seams and press open.

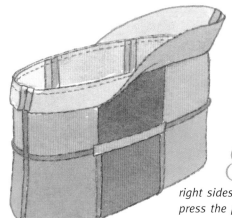

8 Attach the top panel, with the right sides together. Trim and press the panel upwards.

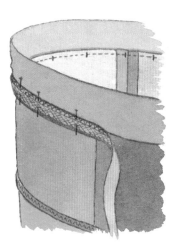

9 Hand stitch the ribbon to the outside top of the bag.

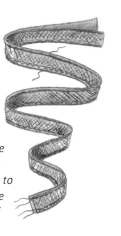

10 Machine stitch 2 lengths of ribbon together to make the handles. Machine stitch along both edges of the handles. Repeat for second handle.

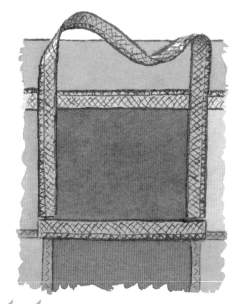

11 Attach the ribbon handles to the outside of the bag using catch stitch.

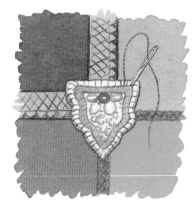

12 Hand stitch the decorative motifs into position.

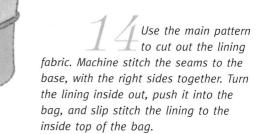

14 Use the main pattern to cut out the lining fabric. Machine stitch the seams to the base, with the right sides together. Turn the lining inside out, push it into the bag, and slip stitch the lining to the inside top of the bag.

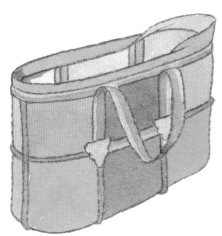

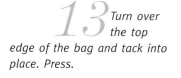

13 Turn over the top edge of the bag and tack into place. Press.

MATERIALS AND EQUIPMENT

- 46cm (18 in) gold satin (standard width 90cm/36 in)
- 46cm (18 in) black lace (standard width 90cm/36 in)
- 23cm (9 in) black lining (standard width 90cm/36 in)
- 23cm (9 in) buckram (standard width 90cm/36 in)
- 23cm (9 in) Domette (standard width 90cm/36 in)
- 46cm (18 in) Petersham ribbon (12mm/ ½ in wide)
- 90cm (36 in) beaded ribbon
- 46cm (18 in) bias binding
- 1 hair band
- 1 large silk rose
- 2 small roses
- Black and gold feather trim
- Matching threads
- Florist's wire
- Fabric glue

*t*his fabulous flower, feather, bead and lace bag is a work of art in its own right. Admirers will never guess that the design was inspired by a humble flower pot! Easy to make, yet ever so sophisticated, this evening bag was created without a sewing machine.

belle *époque*

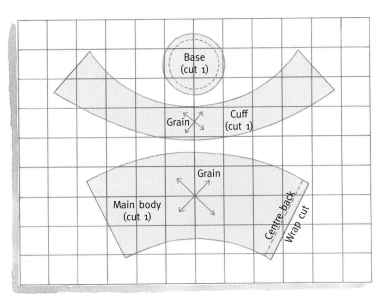

1 square equals 5cm (2 in)

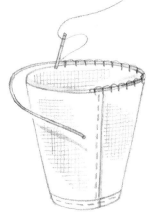

1 Use the pattern to cut out all the shapes from the buckram fabric leaving 2.5cm (1 inch) seam allowance. Take the buckram for the main bag and overlap the back by 1cm (³⁄₈ inch). Tack and stitch together with running stitch.

2 Take some medium-weight florist's wire and use blanket stitch to attach it to the top edge of the bag. Cut a strip of bias binding 40cm (16 inches) long. Place it over the raw edges of the bag, top and bottom, and tack it into place.

3 For the cuff, use blanket stitch to sew some medium-weight florist wire along the side edges and the bottom.

4 Bind all four edges of the cuff with bias binding, snipping and mitering the corners.

5 For the lining, use the pattern to cut out all the shapes from the domette. Cut on the bias, leaving a 2.5cm (1 in) seam allowance.

6 Cover both shapes with domette, butting rather than overlapping the edges at the back of the bag. Trim off the seam allowance at the join and whip stitch to secure.

7 Turn over the surplus domette, top and bottom, for both the cuff and the bag.

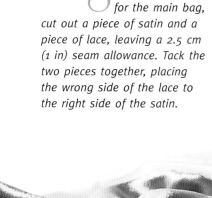

8 Using the pattern for the main bag, cut out a piece of satin and a piece of lace, leaving a 2.5 cm (1 in) seam allowance. Tack the two pieces together, placing the wrong side of the lace to the right side of the satin.

9 Fold in half and, with the right sides together, hand stitch the back join with a slip stitch, using a fine needle. Trim and press open.

10 Place the fabric over the main body of the bag and pull it into position. Turn the seam allowance at the top and bottom up into the bag, and glue it to the insides.

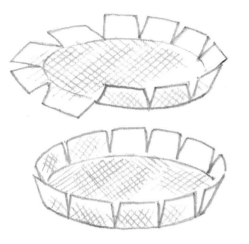

11 Take the base and snip into the seam allowance at intervals. Turn up the snipped seam.

12 Cover the base with domette. Repeat with the satin and lace.

13 Slip the base into the main body of the bag, 5mm (¼ in) from the bottom edge. Use large running stitches to secure it in place. Make sure that the stitches are hidden within the lace pattern.

14 Using the cuff pattern, cut out one piece of satin and one piece of black lining, leaving a 2.5cm (1 in) seam allowance. Place the satin over the domette. Turn under the seam allowance on both sides and the base, and glue to the reverse side.

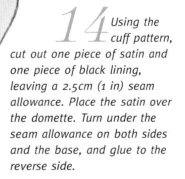

15 Attach the lining to the inside of the cuff. Trim and turn under the seam allowance, securing with a hem stitch. Trim the lining along the top edge, almost to the edge of the buckram.

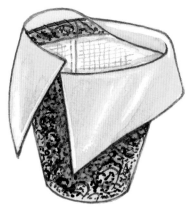

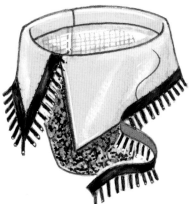

16 Attach the main cuff to the bag using whip stitch along the top edge.

17 Fold the top of the satin cuff over to the inside of the bag, gluing the edge down to secure it.

18 Use a slip stitch to attach the beaded ribbon to the outer edge of the cuff, taking care to miter the corners.

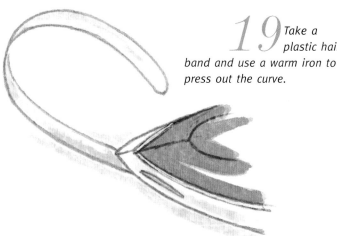

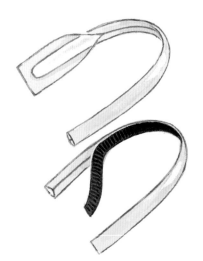

19 Take a plastic hair band and use a warm iron to press out the curve.

20 Cover the hair band with a bias strip of satin and glue together the long edges down the inside of the hair band. Glue a strip of ribbon over the join.

23 Decorate with assorted flowers and feathers of your choice.

22 Cut out the lining to the main pattern. Hand stitch the centre back join and base of the lining, and slip stitch it to the top inside of the bag.

21 Attach the hair band to the inside of the bag with a catch stitch.

*M*ade of waterproof mesh with coloured leather trimmings, this bag has a stylish utilitarian feel, and its foldaway central flap cover makes it practical for all-weather use. You can vary the decoration according to taste: for a different look, use felt instead of leather for the trimmings, and try geometrical shapes with bright or seasonal colours.

all
meshed
up

MATERIALS AND EQUIPMENT

- 80cm (32 in) opaque mesh (standard width 90cm/36 in)
- 12.5cm (5 in) red leather (standard width 140cm/54 in)
- 12.5cm (5 in) green leather (standard width 140cm/54 in)
- Ruler or tape measure
- Clicking knife or scalpel
- Cutting board
- Awl
- Double-sided carpet tape
- Pinking shears
- Scissors

1 square equals 5cm (2 in)

Facing (cut 2) — Grain

Handle position

Main body (cut 1) — Grain

Flap (cut 1) — Grain — Place to fold

Base line

Place to fold of fabric

1 Use the pattern to cut out the main bag, flap cover panel and facing from the mesh material, adding an 2.5cm (1 in) for the seams. Cut out the leather handles: two strips 55cm x 5cm (22 in x 2 in) from the red and 55cm x 2.5cm (22 in x 1 in) from the green. Make the flower stems from thinner strips of green leather, and the flower heads from red leather cut in circles with the pinking shears.

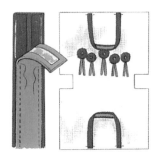

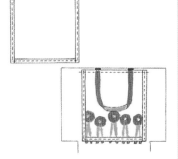

2 Tie a knot in the middle of each stem. Pierce the centre of each flower head with the awl and fix two pieces of carpet tape on the back. Run both the stem ends through the hole in the flower head so that the knot shows on the right side, then fix carpet tape to the back of the stems.

3 Position the flowers on the front of the bag using the tape to hold them in position. Machine stitch a single line up one strand of the stem and down the other, holding the head out of the way.

4 Make the handles by folding the red pieces over lengthways so they meet in the middle. Fix a strip of carpet tape to the back of each piece of green leather. Press this down on the back of the red pieces so the join is completely covered, and machine stitch. Pin in position on the bag and machine stich.

5 Neaten the edges of the inside flap cover by turning over 1cm (³⁄₈ in) seam allowance on three sides, wrong sides together, leaving the top edge unturned. Machine stitch. Place over the centre of the front body of the bag right sides together, with the unturned edge at the top, and machine stitch just above the seam line, 1cm (³⁄₈ in) from the edge.

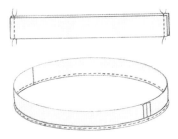

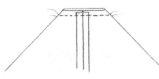

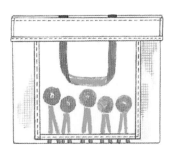

6 Make the facing by sewing the two strips right sides together at their narrow edges. Turn up the hem wrong sides facing 1cm (³⁄₈ in) at the bottom and machine stitch all around it.

7 With right sides of the front and back body of the bag together, sew up the side seams. Fold out the bottom of the bag, making sure the centre of the base falls in line with the side seams, and machine stitch along the base on both sides.

8 Turn the bag right side out and position the facing along the top edge, right sides together, with the unturned edge of the facing to the top of the bag. Machine stitch on the seam line all around the top of the facing and bag.

9 Turn back the facing to the inside of the bag and machine stitch all around 1cm (³⁄₈ in) from the top to give a firm, straight edge. Trim all thread ends to finish.

MATERIALS AND EQUIPMENT

- 50cm (20 in) corduroy furnishing fabric (standard width 140cm/54 in)
- 50cm (20 in) lining material (standard width 90cm/36 in)
- 50cm (20 in) iron-on interfacing (standard width 90cm/36 in)
- 80cm (30 in) decorative braid
- 10cm (4 in) suedette or felt (standard width 140cm/54 in)
- 30cm x 8cm (12 in x 3 in) piece of corrugated plastic card
- 6 brass studs
- Matching threads
- Pinking shears
- Scissors

*t*ough and versatile, corduroy furnishing fabric is perfect for a hard-wearing tote bag. The suedette patches lift the design, making it more individual. Here, the bag is a neutral colour, however you could make a bolder statement in red, pink or orange, or a sleekly sophisticated version in black and grey.

carried away

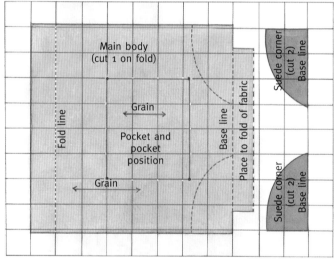

1 square equals 5cm (2 in)

1 Use the pattern to cut out the corduroy fabric for the main bag, adding an extra 2.5cm (1 in) for the seams. Cut out the iron-on interfacing to the same pattern and iron on to the wrong side of the main bag fabric.

2 Cut out the corner patches in suede, using pinking shears on the curved edges.

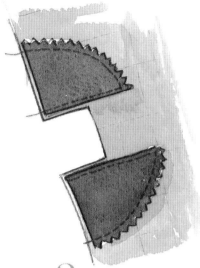

3 Pin, tack and stitch the suede corners to the cord fabric as shown above.

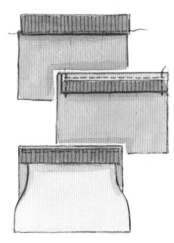

4 Cut out the cord pocket using the pattern. Machine stitch the cotton tape along the top edge of the pocket. Fold the tape down onto the right side. Machine stitch down the two short edges of the tape. Trim and turn through.

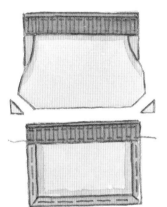

5 Miter the corners of the pocket to prevent bulkiness. Turn the seam in on three sides. Machine stitch along the bottom edge of the tape.

6 Pin, tack and stitch the pocket to the bag. Machine a double row of stitching around all three sides of the pocket.

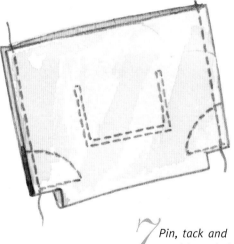

7 Pin, tack and machine stitch the side seams of the main bag, with the right sides together. Trim the seams and press open.

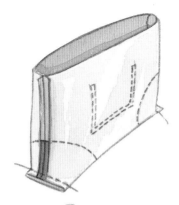

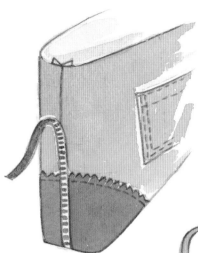

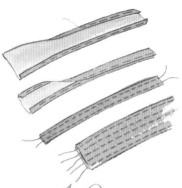

8 Tack and machine stitch the bottom edge of the side panel to the base. Repeat for the other side panel. Turn through to the right side.

9 An optional feature would be to cover the side seams with a piece of decorative braid. Slip stitch into place.

10 Fold 5mm (¼ in) along each long edge of the handle fabric. Bring the two folded edges together. Tack into place and machine stitch along both long edges. Then machine another three rows of stitching between the two outer rows.

11 Pin the handles to the top edge of the bag. Tack and stitch two rows into place.

12 Turn over the top of the bag to make an automatic facing 10cm (4 in) in from the top. Machine a row of stitching around the top of the bag.

13 Cut out a piece of corrugated plastic board 5mm (¼ in) smaller than the central section of the template. Mark the positions of the base studs. Using a leather punch, punch out 6 stud holes. Drop the plastic board into the bag.

14 *Push a pin through* each stud hole from the inside to show the position of the stud. Push the stud through the bottom from the outside, where the pin pokes through. Inside the bag, open up the stud prongs over the board.

15 *Using the template, make up the lining* 2mm (⅟₁₂ in) smaller than the main bag. Sew the side and bottom seams. Drop in the lining and slip stitch 2.5cm (1 in) away from the top edge.

MATERIALS AND EQUIPMENT

- 50cm (20 in) Indian silk
  (standard width 90cm/36 in)
- 50cm (20 in) wadding interlining
- 50cm (20 in) Vylene
- 1m (3 ft) plastic tubing
- 1m (3 ft) novelty crinolyn tubing
- 26cm (10 in) zip
- Craft knife
- Cutting board
- Dressmaker's carbon paper
- Matching threads
- Scissors

pretty in pink

*S*hopping bags needn't be drab and boring, as this vibrant silk shopper shows. The luxurious quilting and pretty sheen of the pink silk will survive the most critical of shop assistant's scrutinies. And once you have mastered the quilting technique, no fabric will be safe!

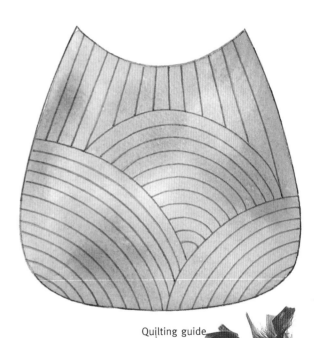

Quilting guide

1 Cut a square of silk, wadding and Vylene 2.5cm (1 in) larger than the pattern, for the back, sides and front of the bag.

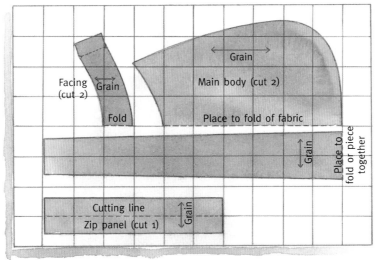

Facing (cut 2)

Grain

Fold

Grain

Main body (cut 2)

Place to fold of fabric

Grain

Place to fold or piece together

Cutting line

Zip panel (cut 1)

Grain

1 square equals 5cm (2 in)

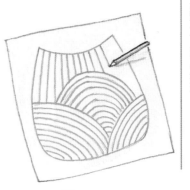

2 Mark up the quilting lines on the Vylene, as shown on the quilting guide. Use carbon paper to transfer your design to the Vylene.

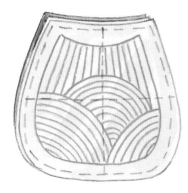

3 Sandwich the wadding between the silk and the Vylene. Tack through the materials, as shown above.

4 Working with the wrong side up, quilt the fabric pieces using a straight stitch on the machine. Remove the tacking stitches.

5 Place the pattern back onto the quilted fabric and cut, leaving a 2cm (¾ in) seam allowance.

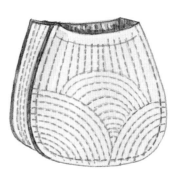

6 Keeping right sides together, place the front to the side. Tack and stitch into place. Repeat for the back, attaching the back to the sides. Remove the tacking stitches.

7 Trim the seam allowance to 5mm (¼ in) and press. To hold the seam in place, catch stitch the seam allowance to the interfacing.

8 Take 20 in (50cm) of plastic tubing and slip it into the novelty crinolyn. Pull the crinolyn over the tube, and finish and stitch the ends, holding the tube in place. Trim off excess crinolyn.

9 Bring the tube ends together and stitch the two ends to form a circle.

10 Cut two strips of silk material 6cm (2½ in) wide by 6cm (2½ in) long, on the bias. Iron on some woven interfacing, cut on the bias, to strengthen the strips. Fold the two edges to meet in the centre. Wrap this over the joined ends of the handle loops, to conceal the join. Tack in place.

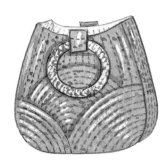

11 Attach the handles to the bag at the centre. Tack and machine stitch them into place.

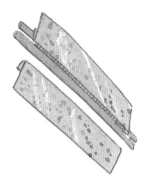

12 Using your pattern, cut out the zip placket. Fold in the turnings along the two edges of the material. Pin and tack the zip along one long edge. Then tack the other piece of material onto the other side of the zip.

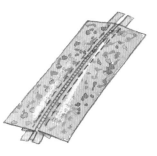

13 Using a zip foot, machine the zip into place. Machine stitch another row of stitches 5mm (¼ in) in from the zip edge, to hold the zip tape in place. Remove all the tacking stitches.

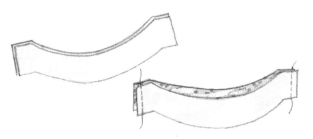

14 Cut the facing material from the silk, using the pattern. Add an extra 2.5cm (1 in) for the seam. Iron some medium-weight iron-on interfacing to the facing material. With the right sides together, machine stitch the side seams. Trim and press open.

15 Attach the zip placket to the facing by tacking and machine stitching along the lower edge of the facing (match the notches). Remove the tacking and trim the seam.

16 Keeping the right sides together, place the facing on the bag. Tack along the top edge. Then, using a piping foot, machine stitch around the top of the bag. Trim and turn facing through to the inside of the bag. Remove the tacking stitches.

o wild with this unusual cheetah print bowling bag made from furnishing fabric. You may find that the fabric styles in the furnishing section are better suited to bag designs, especially those that are going to see a certain amount of wear and tear. If you have enough fabric left over, why not make a matching purse?

bowled over

MATERIALS AND EQUIPMENT

- 40cm (16 in) animal print furnishing fabric (standard width 140cm/54 in)
- 40cm (16 in) matching lining (standard width 90cm/36 in)
- 40cm (16 in) iron-on interfacing (standard width 90cm/36 in)
- 11cm x 20cm (4⅓ in x 8 in) corrugated plastic board
- 1m (3 ft) leather cord
- 46cm (18 in) open-ended zip
- 15cm (6 in) fine leather cord
- 1 brass toggle end
- Matching thread
- Craft knife
- Cutting board
- Scissors

1 Use the pattern to cut out the pieces of fabric for the main bag, adding an extra 2.5cm (1 in) for the seams. Cut out the iron-on interfacing for all pieces using the same pattern.

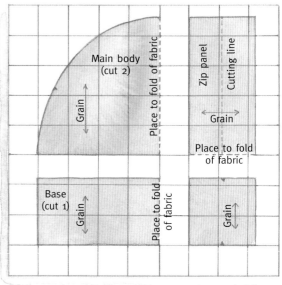

Main body (cut 2)

Grain

Place to fold of fabric

Zip panel

Cutting line

Grain

Place to fold of fabric

Base (cut 1)

Grain

Place to fold of fabric

Grain

1 square equals 5cm (2 in)

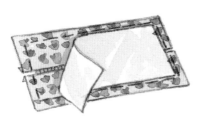

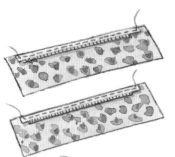

2 Using an open-ended zip, pin and tack it onto the right side of the placket fabric. Machine along the stitch line and trim the seam allowance. Fold over to the right side. Repeat for the other side of the zip. Zip the two pieces together.

3 Place the pattern for the zip placket centrally over the zip and mark the new seam lines.

4 Keeping the right sides together, stitch the two end sections of the placket to both ends. Trim the seam allowance and press.

5 To make the handles, cut some leather cord in half (about 50cm/18 in for each handle). Cut the ends diagonally using a craft knife.

6 Fold the handle fabric down the long edges. Wrap around the leather piping. Using a double thread, whip stitch the two folded edges together.

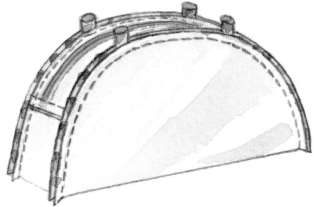

7 Place the handles to the side panels of the bag (the position is marked on the template). Tack into place. With the right sides and matching notches together, tack and stitch the side panels to the zip placket. Trim excess material and remove tacking stitches.

Tip: Avoid sewing over the leather cord, as this may break your machine.

8 Turn the bag back to the right side. Tack the seam allowance to hold in place.

9 Using your base pattern, cut a piece of corrugated card 5mm (¼ in) smaller than the original pattern. Place the card onto the fabric for the base.

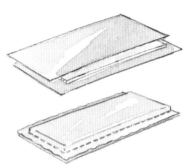

10 Tack a piece of lining on top of the card and tack around the edge. Using a piping foot, stitch around all sides as close to the card as possible. Remove the tacking stitches.

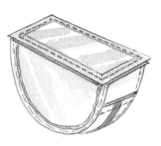

11 Keeping the right sides together, tack and stitch the base to the main bag. Trim any excess seam allowance and turn through to the right side.

Tip: Keep the zip open to ensure you can turn the bag through.

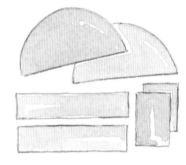

12 Using the pattern, cut out the lining pieces 2mm (¹⁄₁₂ in) smaller than the main bag, adding a seam allowance.

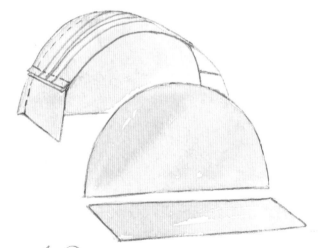

13 Begin by lining the zip placket. Turn in the long edges of the lining piece and tack and machine stitch into place. Then add on the end sections of the zip placket and then the side sections of the bag. Finish off by adding the base piece of the lining.

14 Place the lining into the bag and slip stitch it to the zip tape.

Variation

To make a drawstring purse

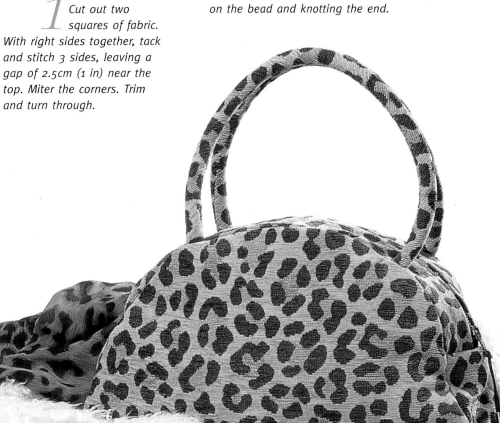

2 Turn over and stitch along the top edge to form a casing for the leather cords. Thread 2 leather cords through the casing, in opposite directions. Finish ends by knotting the cord, threading on the bead and knotting the end.

1 Cut out two squares of fabric. With right sides together, tack and stitch 3 sides, leaving a gap of 2.5cm (1 in) near the top. Miter the corners. Trim and turn through.

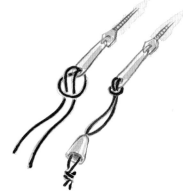

15 To make the zip tab, take a piece of fine leather cord. Loop it over the zip pull. Slide the toggle over the leather cord. Knot the cord, trim and pull the end back into the toggle.

MATERIALS AND EQUIPMENT

- 40cm (16 in) striped silk (standard width 90cm/36 in)
- 40cm (16 in) contrast lining (standard width 90cm/36 in)
- 30cm x 7cm (12 in x 7 in) black lining (standard width 90cm/36 in)
- 1m (3 ft) black webbing
- 80cm (30 in) beaded cord
- 30cm (12 in) and 18cm (7 in) zips
- Matching thread

*t*his jazzy striped silk bag will suit any outfit. It has the full range of rainbow colours, which are also reflected in the beaded side seams. However, you could also use plain silk or taffetta or other patterned fabrics, such as ticking, striped cotton or linen. If you have some fabric left over, why not make a matching purse?

over the rainbow

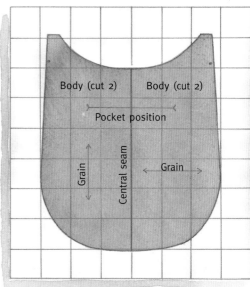

Body (cut 2)   Body (cut 2)

Pocket position

Grain   Central seam   Grain

1 square equals 5cm (2 in)

1 Cut out the silk for the main bag to the pattern, adding an 2.5cm (1 in) for the seams. Cut two sections with vertical stripes and two with horizontal stripes. Cut a length of fabric for the handle, with the stripes running lengthways.

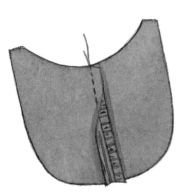

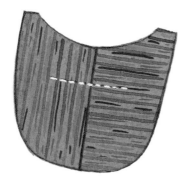

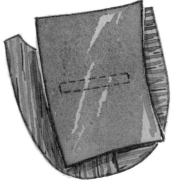

2 Tack and stitch the centre front and centre back seams. Trim and press open. Remove the tacking stitches.

3 To make the pocket lining, cut a piece of black lining fabric 2.5cm x 4cm (1 in x 1½ in). Fold in half and press to mark the centre line.

4 Using the centre line as a guide, place the lining over the right side of the back section. Then tack along the centre, using a zip foot. Stitch down both lengths of the tacking, and across both ends. Remove the tacking stitches.

5 With a sharp pair of scissors, cut along the fold line and into the corners. Turn through to the wrong side and tack along the stitched edge.

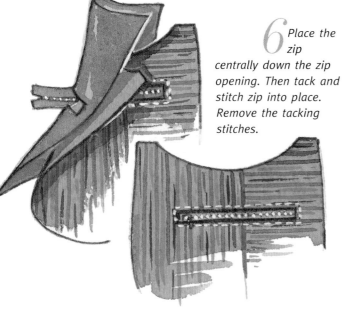

6 Place the zip centrally down the zip opening. Then tack and stitch zip into place. Remove the tacking stitches.

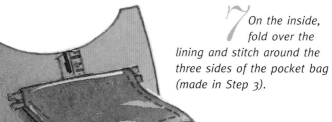

7 On the inside, fold over the lining and stitch around the three sides of the pocket bag (made in Step 3).

8 *Cut out the lining fabric for the main bag using the pattern. Keeping the right sides together, tack and stitch the two pieces of lining to the top edge of the bag. Trim and turn through. Tack around the curved edge.*

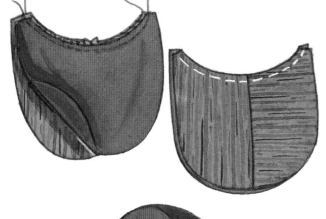

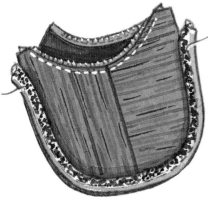

9 *Unzip the main zip. Pin and tack each side of the zip to the front and back of the bag. Machine stitch in place using a zip foot. Remove the tacking stitches.*

10 *Tack the beaded braid around the outer edge of the main bag material.*

11 *Place the right sides of the main fabric together. Pin and tack around the whole bag, using a piping foot. Machine stitch the fabric to the points where the braid exits at the top of the side seams.*

12 *To add the strap, fold and tack the pre-cut strap fabric down the two long edges. Place the webbing on top. Tack and machine stitch down the two long edges. Remove the tacking stitches.*

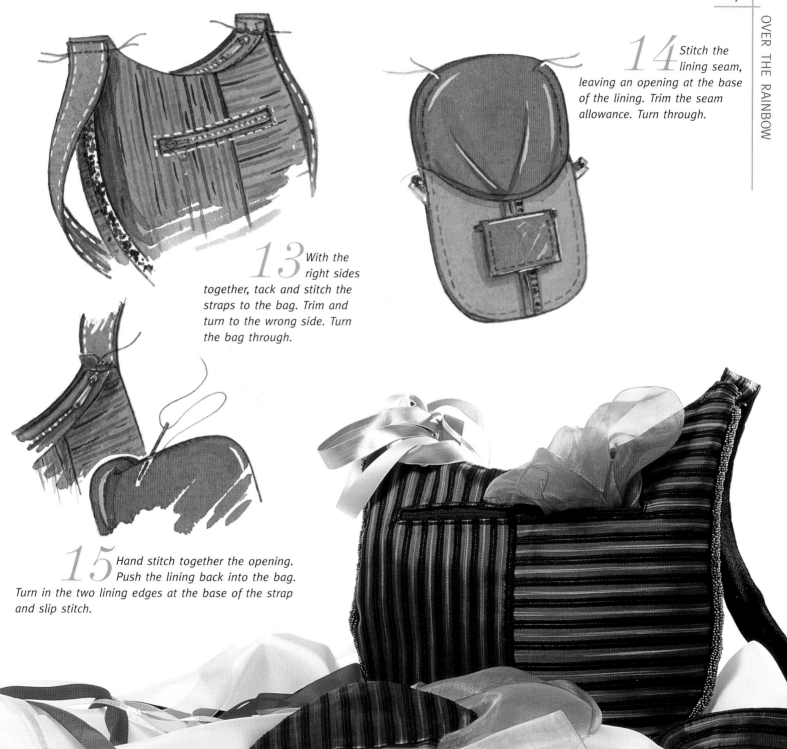

14 Stitch the lining seam, leaving an opening at the base of the lining. Trim the seam allowance. Turn through.

13 With the right sides together, tack and stitch the straps to the bag. Trim and turn to the wrong side. Turn the bag through.

15 Hand stitch together the opening. Push the lining back into the bag. Turn in the two lining edges at the base of the strap and slip stitch.

little
red pony

*t*he witty pony pattern and soft panne velvet of this roomy shopper give it a jazzy edge over shop-bought bags. You'll find that a simple shape can be the best option if you have a wild pattern that you want to show off to its best advantage. There's no need to use real leather for the side panels – here, a mock snake fabric works just as well.

MATERIALS AND EQUIPMENT

- 50cm (20 in) panne velvet, pony pattern (standard width 140cm/54 in)
- 10cm (4 in) black mock snake material (standard width 140cm/54 in)
- 50cm (20 in) lining fabric (standard width 90cm/36 in)
- 1.5m (60 in) black leather piping

- 6 studs
- Corrugated plastic board 40cm x 8cm (15 in x 3 in)
- 50cm (20 in) iron-on interfacing (standard width 90cm/36 in)
- 36cm (14 in) zip
- Matching threads
- Pinking shears
- Scissors

Piping point

Place to fold of the fabric

Base line

Facing cutting line

Main body (cut 1)

Grain

Piping point

Zip tab

Grain

Side panel (cut 2)

Cutting line

Zip panel (cut 2)

1 square equals 5cm (2 in)

1 Fold the panne velvet in half lengthwise. Use the pattern to cut out the main bag, adding an extra 2.5cm (1 in) for the seams. Cut out the mock snake leather sections, adding extra seam allowance. Cut out the iron-on interfacing to the pattern, and iron it onto the velvet and mock leather.

2 Tack the leather piping around the sides of the bag beginning and ending at the point marked on the pattern.

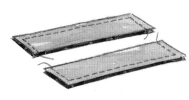

3 Take the mock leather side panels and fold over the top edge by 1 cm (¼ in). With the right sides together, tack and stitch the side panels to the main bag. Trim and remove tacking stitches.

4 Keeping the right sides together, attach a piece of lining to each section of the zip placket. Stitch along one long edge and the two short ends. Repeat for other side of the zip. Trim and turn through.

5 Place the zip centrally over the right side of the zip placket. Stitch along the long edges using a zip foot, as close to the zip teeth as possible.

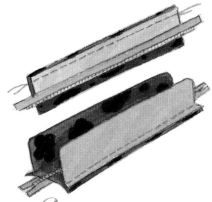

6 With right sides together, place the zip plackets to the bag facing. Stitch along the tacking line and trim. Repeat for the opposite facing. Remove all the tacking stitches.

7 To make the handles, cut two mock leather strips using the pattern. Iron the interfacing to the wrong side. Fold both long edges into the wrong side and tack into place.

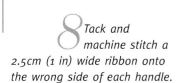

8 Tack and machine stitch a 2.5cm (1 in) wide ribbon onto the wrong side of each handle.

9 Keeping the right sides together, place the handles on the top edge of the bag, as marked on the pattern. Tack into place.

10 Undo the zip and attach the facing to the main bag, with the right sides together. Machine stitch along the top edge, curving down to the top of the mock leather side panels. Turn over and tack around the outer edge.

11 Cut a rectangle 40cm x 8cm (15 in x 3 in) from corrugated plastic board. Mark the positions of the base studs. Using a leather punch, punch out 6 stud holes. Drop the plastic board into the base of the bag.

12 Push a pin through each stud hole to mark the position of the stud. Push the stud through the bottom, right side, where each pin emerges through the fabric. Open up the stud prongs over the board, inside the bag, to secure it in place.

13 Machine stitch over the original stitching line holding the facing and zip together.

15 Fold in the turnings and slip stitch along the zip placket, and sides.

14 Make up a lining from pieces cut using the pattern, just 2mm (¹⁄₁₂ in) smaller, but remember to leave some seam allowance. Tack and machine stitch together. Drop the lining into the bag.

16 Cut four crescent-shaped tabs using the template. Place over the zip ends. Tack and stitch into place. Trim close to stitching line and remove all tacking stitches.

*U*se offcuts of fabric left over from sewing cushions, curtains and clothes to make a colourful appliquéd bag for more informal occasions. You can create some really interesting combinations of texture, pattern and colour if you experiment.

floral *appliqué*

1 *Using the pattern, cut out all the pieces for the main bag, adding an extra 2.5cm (1 in) for the seams. Cut out all the pieces in the interfacing material and iron them on to the wrong side of the main parts of the bag.*

MATERIALS AND EQUIPMENT

- 30cm (12 in) floral fabric (standard width 90cm/36 in)
- Offcuts of velvet, spotted fabric, turquoise fabric and slubbed silk
- 30cm (12 in) piece of lining (standard width 90cm/36 in)
- 10cm (4 in) Bondaweb
- 1m (40 in) plastic ribbon
- 30cm (12 in) iron-on light-weight interfacing (standard width 90cm/36 in)
- 10cm (4 in) medium weight iron-on interfacing (standard width 90cm/36 in)
- 15cm x 25cm (6 in x 10 in) corrugated plastic card
- Matching threads
- Scissors

Base (cut 1)	Main body (cut 2)	Cuff (cut 2)	Facing (cut 2)
←Grain→	←Grain→	←Grain→	←Grain→
Place to fold	Place to fold of fabric	Fold	Fold

1 square equals 5cm (2 in)

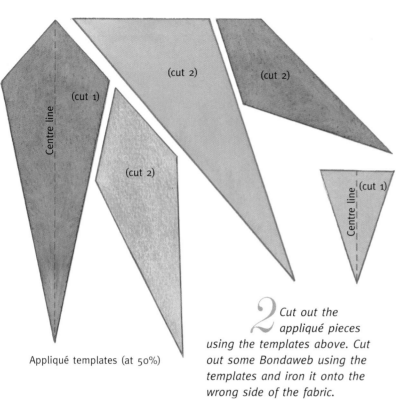

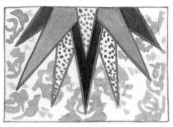

Centre line (cut 1)

(cut 2)

(cut 2)

(cut 2)

(cut 2)

Centre line (cut 1)

Appliqué templates (at 50%)

2 Cut out the appliqué pieces using the templates above. Cut out some Bondaweb using the templates and iron it onto the wrong side of the fabric.

3 Pin, tack and machine stitch the patches onto the main bag using a close zigzag stitch (twice), following the order shown above. Remove all pins and tacking stitches.

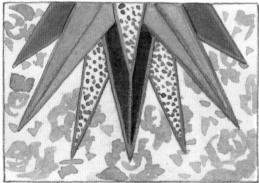

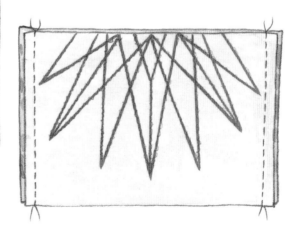

4 Add a decorative zigzag machine stitch to the centre of the last three panels.

5 With the right sides together, tack and machine stitch together the side seams of the main bag. Trim and press the seams open.

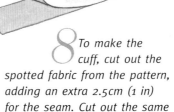

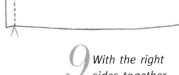

6 For the base of the bag, take the corrugated plastic card and sandwich it between the base fabric and the iron-on interfacing. Iron around the edges, using a low heat.

7 With the right sides together, tack and machine stitch the base to the bag. Remove all tacking stitches and snip into the corners.

8 To make the cuff, cut out the spotted fabric from the pattern, adding an extra 2.5cm (1 in) for the seam. Cut out the same amount of medium-weight fusible interfacing, and iron on.

9 With the right sides together, machine stitch the side seams of the cuff. Trim and press open.

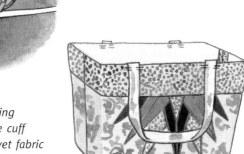

10 With the right sides together, place the cuff and the main bag seams together. Tack and stitch into place. Remove all tacking stitches. Trim and press open.

11 Using the cuff pattern, cut some velvet fabric for the facing, adding an extra 2.5cm (1 in) for the seams. Repeat Step 10. Trim and press the seams open.

12 Cut the plastic ribbon in half. Position the handles on the top of the bag, 12cm (5 in) away from the side seams. Tack into place.

13 With the right sides together, position the facing on the bag. Tack and hand stitch in place. Remove all tacking stitches. Trim the seam allowance and turn through to the right side.

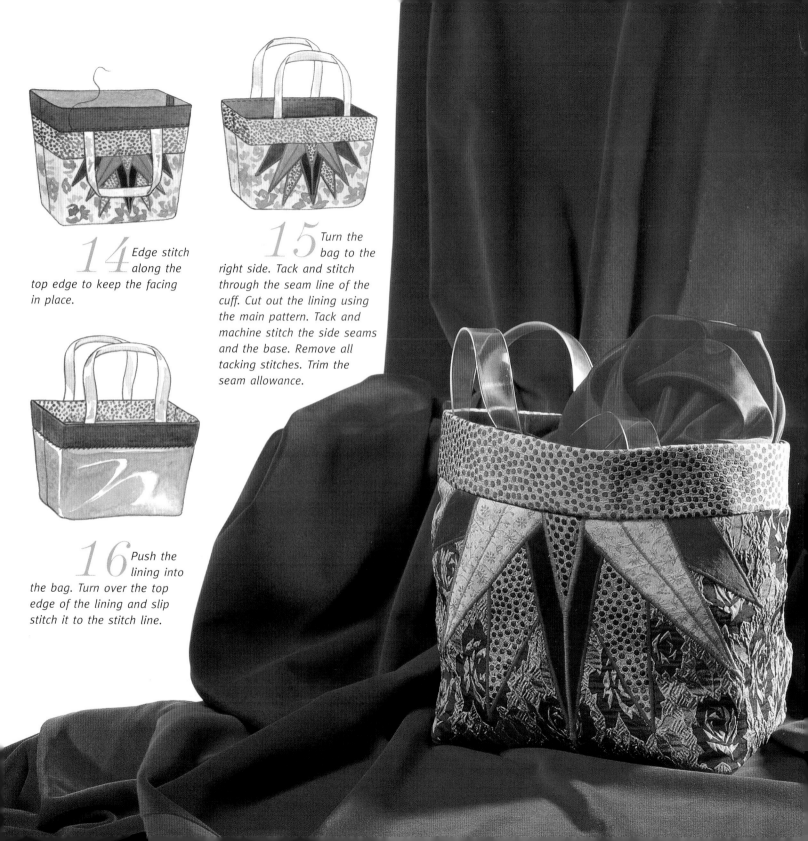

14 Edge stitch along the top edge to keep the facing in place.

15 Turn the bag to the right side. Tack and stitch through the seam line of the cuff. Cut out the lining using the main pattern. Tack and machine stitch the side seams and the base. Remove all tacking stitches. Trim the seam allowance.

16 Push the lining into the bag. Turn over the top edge of the lining and slip stitch it to the stitch line.

MATERIALS AND EQUIPMENT

- 30cm (20 in) fake fur fabric (standard width 140cm/54 in)
- 20cm (8 in) leather or mock leather piece (standard width 140cm/54 in)
- 30cm (20 in) matching lining (standard width 90cm/36 in)

- 3m (3 ft) leather wrapped cord
- 26cm (10 in) zip
- Matching thread
- Leather needle
- Sticky tape
- Craft knife
- Cutting board
- Scissors

Davy Crockett

*W*itty and tactile, this Davy Crockett shoulder bag will turn heads wherever you go. The rough texture of the fake fur begs to be stroked, and the unusual leather cord handle and leather fringing give the bag that Wild West touch.

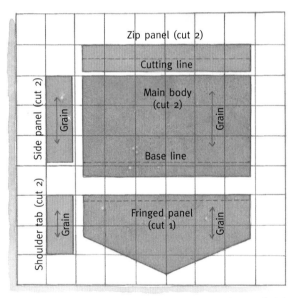

1 square equals 5cm (2 in)

1 Use the pattern to cut out the fake fur fabric for the back and front of the main bag, adding an extra 2.5cm (1 in) for the seam allowance. For the leather sections, place the pattern right side up on the leather skin.

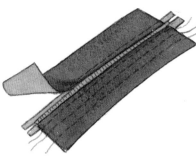

2 Lay the two strips of leather down the length of the zip. Tack and machine stitch into place. Stitch two more rows an equal distance from the first row.

3 Place your pattern back on top of the zip and tack around the original seam allowance.

4 Working on the wrong side of the bottom piece of leather, use a pen and ruler to draw lines an equal distance apart. Carefully cut up the lines to within 12mm (½ in) of the top.

5 Place the leather side of the fringe to the right side of the fake fur. Tack along one edge.

6 Attach second piece of fake fur, sandwiching the leather fringe between the two right sides of the fur. Machine stitch along the tacking line, using a leather needle in your machine.

7 With leather side to the right side of the fake fur, tack and stitch the side seams of the side panels to the main bag. Then tack and stitch the base seam.

8 To make the handle loops, cut two 50cm (20 in) lengths from the 3m (3 ft) of leather wrapped cord. Tack one to the top of each side panel, with the cut edges facing upwards.

Tip: Before you cut the braid, bind the area you are going to cut with sticky tape. Cut through the centre (this will prevent it from unravelling).

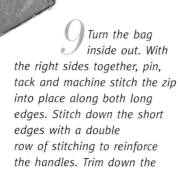

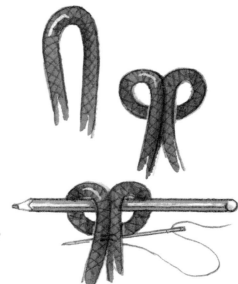

9 Turn the bag inside out. With the right sides together, pin, tack and machine stitch the zip into place along both long edges. Stitch down the short edges with a double row of stitching to reinforce the handles. Trim down the seam allowance.

10 Take the cord handle loops that you stitched into the bag (Step 8). Turn over the end loop, and slide through a pencil or pen to hold into place while stitching the loop to the cord.

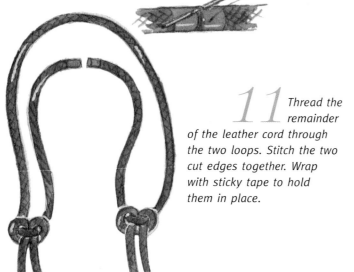

11 Thread the remainder of the leather cord through the two loops. Stitch the two cut edges together. Wrap with sticky tape to hold them in place.

12 From the remaining leather, cut two rectangles using the shoulder guard template. On one piece, turn in 5mm (¼ in) of the shorter edges onto the wrong side of the leather.

13 Place the wrong side of the smaller piece onto the right side of the larger piece, and machine stitch down the centre.

15 Cut the lining fabric to the main bag pattern. Tack and stitch all seams together. Place the lining into the bag and attach it with a slip stitch to the top seam line.

14 Slip the two cords onto the leather shoulder guard. Tack, and using a piping foot, machine stitch as close to the cord as possible. Trim off any excess leather as close to the stitching line as possible.

16 Place the lining into the bag and attach it with a slip stitch to the top seam line.

spring
flowers

f inding a hard-wearing bag in a light style with delicate detailing would normally be a tough task. However, if you combine see-through mesh with mock leather furnishing fabric, and apply a few tricks of the trade, you will have a smart bag to take you through spring to summer.

MATERIALS AND EQUIPMENT

- 40cm (16 in) mock leather furnishing fabric (standard width 140cm/54 in)
- 40cm x 40cm (16 in x 16 in) piece of white crinolyn (standard width 90cm/36 in)
- 2 "D" rings
- Rainbow thread
- Matching thread
- Leather needle
- Magnet catch
- Craft knife
- Cutting board
- Scissors

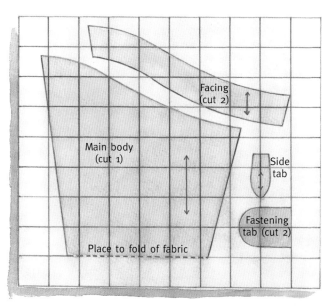

Facing (cut 2)

Main body (cut 1)

Side tab

Fastening tab (cut 2)

Place to fold of fabric

1 square equals 5cm (2 in)

1 Use the pattern to cut out the mock leather fabric for the main bag. Note that the leatherette needs to be folded in half before cutting. Using the same pattern, cut out one layer of crinolyn. Add an extra 2.5cm (1 in) to both leatherette and crinolyn for the seams.

2 Using the template, draw the outline of the cut-out leaf motifs onto the wrong side of the mock leather. Cut out the pattern with a craft knife and cutting board.

Template for
main bag cut-outs

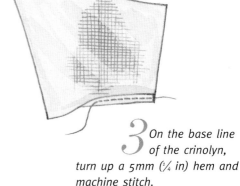

3 On the base line of the crinolyn, turn up a 5mm (¼ in) hem and machine stitch.

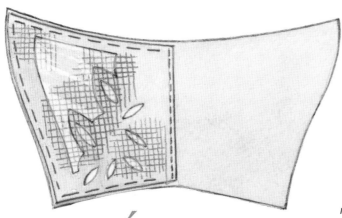

4 Place the wrong side of the crinolyn to the wrong side of the cut leatherette piece. Pin and tack into place.

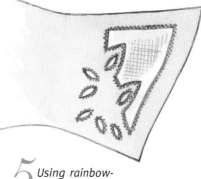

5 Using rainbow-coloured thread, machine on the right side around all the edges of the pattern with a medium close zigzag stitch.

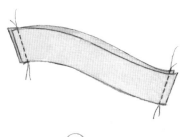

8 Tack and stitch the side seams of the facing material, with right sides together. Trim and neaten.

6 With the right sides of the bag together, tack and machine stitch the side seams. Trim and neaten.

7 Pull the bag through to the wrong side. Flatten the end of the side seam as shown, and machine stitch 2.5cm (1 in) from the pointed end. Trim off any excess material and neaten. Turn the bag through to the right side.

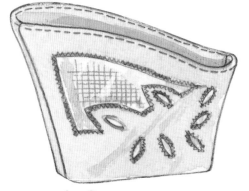

9 Keeping the right sides together, stitch the facing to the top edge of the bag. Trim the seam allowance and turn over to the wrong side.

10 Tack along the top edge and machine a row of stitching. Remove the tacking stitches.

11 Using the template, cut two handle plackets. Fold the end of each placket over a "D" ring and, using a piping foot, stitch as close to the "D" ring as possible.

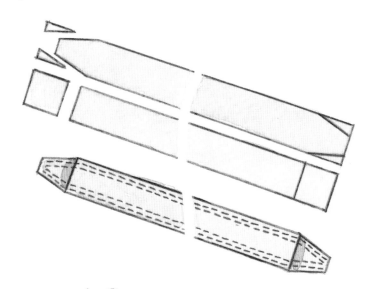

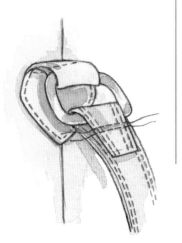

12 Place the placket over the side seam. Tack and stitch into place. Repeat for the second handle placket.

13 Cut two strips of mock leather 1m x 2.5cm (40 in x 1 in) each. Taper each end on one strip only. Trim the other strip to the point of the taper. With the wrong sides together, place the shorter strip on top of the longer one. Machine two rows of stitches all the way around.

14 Slide the tapered end through the "D" ring and fold it back on itself. Stitch securely into place. Repeat with the other end of the strap.

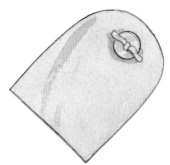

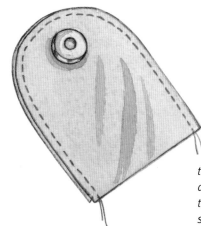

15 For an optional tab to close the bag, cut two pieces of mock leather from the pattern, adding a 2.5cm (1 in) seam. Insert the magnetic fastener to one piece, as shown.

16 With the wrong sides together, tack and stitch around the outer edge of the tabs. Trim close to the machine stitch line.

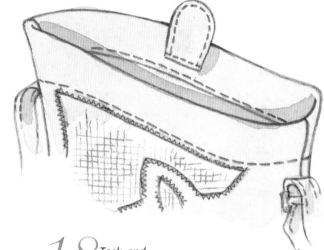

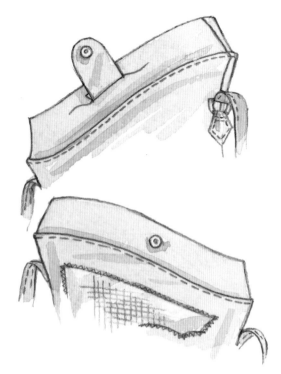

18 Tack and machine stitch the facing into place 2.5cm (1 in) from the top edge. Trim the facing.

17 Place the tab to the centre of the facing, with the right sides together. Tack and make a double row of stitching to hold it in place. On the opposite side, insert a magnetic catch for the fastener.

19 Using the templates, cut out the flower motifs and machine stitch the pattern with rainbow thread and a medium close zigzag stitch.

Tip Start stitching from the centre and move outwards.

Flower templates

Variation

SUN, SEA AND SAND
For a summery feel, change the theme of your bag
with this simple mesh "wave" cut-out and these
shell and starfish motifs. Use a medium close
zigzag stitch with the rainbow thread on the
dotted lines of the motif templates. Attach the
motifs to the bag with a catch stitch.

20 Catch stitch the flower motifs onto the bag.

suppliers list

Sewing Equipment

General Embellishments

The John Lewis Partnership
171 Victoria Street
London
SW1E 5NA
Tel. 020 7828 1000

Sewing machines

Chapel Market Sewing
Centre
17 Chapel Market
Islington
London
N1 9EZ
Tel. 020 7837 5372

Sykes Sewing Machines
5 Castle Street
Edgeley
Stockport
Cheshire
SK3 9AB
Tel. 0161 480 2381

Sewing Materials

Fabric

Cloth House
14 Berwick Street
Soho
London
Tel. 020 7287 2881

Soho Silks
22 D'Arblay Street
London
W1F 8EG
Tel. 020 7434 3305

MacCulloch & Wallis Ltd.
25-26 Dering Street
London
W1R OBH
Tel. 020 7629 0311
www.macculloch-wallis.co.uk

Online Fabrics
388-394 Foleshill Road
Coventry
West Midlands
Tel. 02476 687776
www.online-fabrics.co.uk

Wool

Clarke's for Wools
9 Pound Place
London
SE9 5DN
Tel. 020 8859 6795

Bow Peep
136 Liverpool Road
Longton
Preston
Lancashire
PR4 5AU
Tel. 01772 614508

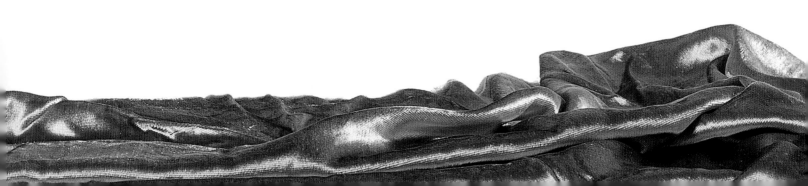

Sewing Embellishments

General Embellishments

The John Lewis Partnership
171 Victoria Street
London
SW1E 5NA
Tel. 020 7828 1000

Klein
5 Nöel Street
London
W1F 8GA
Tel. 020 7437 6162

MacCulloch & Wallis Ltd.
25-26 Dering Street
London
W1R OBH
Tel. 020 7629 0311
www.macculloch-wallis.co.uk

V V Rouleaux
32 Old Burlington Street
London
W1S 3AT
Tel. 020 7434 3899

Beads

London Bead Co.
25 Chalk Farm Road
London
NW1 8AG
Tel. 020 7267 9403

The Northern Bead Co.
Corn Exchange
Leeds
West Yorkshire
Tel. 0113 244 3033

Buttons

The Button Lady
16 Hollyfield Road South
Sutton Coldfield
West Midlands
B76 1NX
Tel. 0121 329 3234
www.thebuttonlady.co.uk

Ribbons

Barnett Lawson Trimmings
16/17 Little Portland Street
London
W1N 6NE
www.bltrimmings.com

Sequins and Braid Specialists

Streamers
Unit 1
Tavistock House
Tavistock Street
Bletchley
Milton Keynes
MK2 2BG
www.streamers.co.uk

Many of the sewing centres listed stock a full range of sewing materials and equipment.

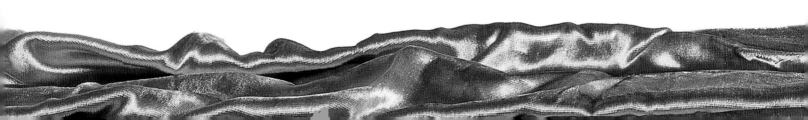

index